FLORIDA Treasures

A Reading/Language Arts Program

Mc Graw Hill **Macmillan/McGraw-Hill**

Contributors

Time Magazine, Accelerated Reader

learning through listening

Students with print disabilities may be eligible to obtain an accessible, audio version of the pupil edition of this textbook. Please call Recording for the Blind & Dyslexic at 1-800-221-4792 for complete information.

B

The *McGraw·Hill* Companies

Macmillan
McGraw-Hill

Published by Macmillan/McGraw-Hill, of McGraw-Hill Education, a division of The McGraw-Hill Companies, Inc., Two Penn Plaza, New York, New York 10121.

Printed in the United States of America

ISBN-13: 978-0-02-198765-8/3, Bk. 2
ISBN-10: 0-02-198765-3/3, Bk. 2
2 3 4 5 6 7 8 9 (079/043) 11 10 09 08

FLORIDA Treasures

A Reading/Language Arts Program

Program Authors

Dr. Donald R. Bear
University of Nevada, Reno
Reno, Nevada

Dr. Janice A. Dole
University of Utah
Salt Lake City, Utah

Dr. Douglas Fisher
San Diego State University
San Diego, California

Dr. Vicki Gibson
Longmire Learning Center, Inc.
College Station, Texas

Dr. Jana Echevarria
California State University, Long Beach
Long Beach, California

Dr. Jan E. Hasbrouck
Educational Consultant - J.H. Consulting
Seattle, Washington

Dr. Scott G. Paris
University of Michigan
Ann Arbor, Michigan

Dr. Timothy Shanahan
University of Illinois at Chicago
Chicago, Illinois

Dr. Josefina V. Tinajero
University of Texas at El Paso
El Paso, Texas

McGraw Hill **Macmillan/McGraw-Hill**

Unit 4 — Determination

4

Award Winning Author

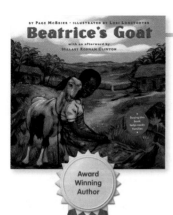

Award Winning Author

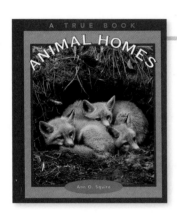

Unit 6

Achievements

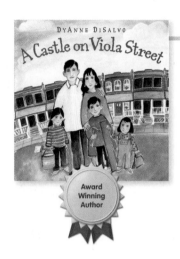

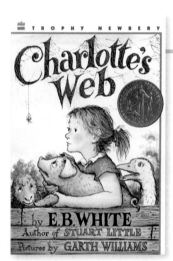

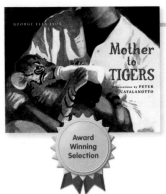
FCAT

What's Cooking?

Red and Her Friends

by Marilyn MacGregor

A hen named Red lived in a city. Red and her pals did everything together. One day, Red and her feline friend Fiona went shopping. As they passed a trash-filled, weed-covered lot, Red smiled. "Wouldn't that lot be a **magnificent** spot for a garden?" she asked.

Fiona didn't see eye to eye with Red. "This place is a mess. It's a disaster!"

"We'd have to clean it up, of course," said Red. She called Ricardo over and asked for help.

"Sorry. I have a dentist appointment," Ricardo barked and walked away wagging his tail.

Red was disappointed. Fiona hissed angrily.

"I'll help you," said Fiona.

Red and Fiona cleaned the lot. Then it was time to plant seeds.

"I wish I could help," said Ricardo, "But I have bones to dig up."

"I'll help," said Fiona, shaking her head at the dog.

Red and Fiona planted beans, carrots, pumpkins, and squash. Soon the seeds grew and made the garden beautiful. It looked like a **masterpiece**! Red asked her friends to help weed and water. Only Fiona had time to help. When it was time to pick the vegetables, only Red and Fiona did the work.

"I'll make dinner," said Red. "Each vegetable will be an **ingredient** in my **recipes** for cooking vegetable stew and pumpkin pie." Red licked her lips. "Those are **tasty** dishes."

Ricardo happened to walk by just then.

"I'd be happy to come to dinner," he said.

"You didn't help clean, weed, water, or pick. What makes you think you're invited?" asked Fiona. Red nodded firmly.

Of course, Fiona was invited, and everything was delicious.

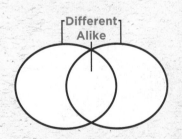

Reread for **Comprehension**

Make Inferences and Analyze

FCAT **Compare Characters** To compare and contrast characters you need to make inferences about how the characters are **alike** and **different**. As you read, think about each character's actions, traits, and feelings. Then ask yourself how they are alike and different. A Venn Diagram can help you compare characters. Reread the selection to compare Fiona with Ricardo.

Different
Alike

Comprehension

Genre

Humorous Fiction is a made-up story written to make the reader laugh.

Make Inferences and Analyze

FCAT **Compare Characters**

As you read, use your Venn Diagram.

Different
Alike

Read to Find Out

Who will help Rooster bake a strawberry shortcake?

14

Cook-a-Doodle-Doo!

by Janet Stevens and
Susan Stevens Crummel
illustrated by Janet Stevens

Award
Winning
Selection

Peck. Peck. Peck.

"Always chicken feed! Day after day—year after year—I'm sick of it!" squawked Big Brown Rooster. "Can we get something new to eat around here? Please? Nobody's listening. What's a hungry rooster to do?"

"There's no hope. Wait a minute … " Rooster remembered a story his mama used to tell, a story handed down from chicken to chicken. The story of his famous great-grandmother, the Little Red Hen.

Rooster rushed into the chicken coop. "It has to be here," he said. He looked high and low, and there it was at last, hidden under a nest—her cookbook. *The Joy of Cooking Alone* by L. R. Hen.

Rooster carefully turned the pages. "So many **recipes**—and I thought she just baked bread! Look at the strawberry shortcake!"

"That's it! I'll make the most wonderful, **magnificent** strawberry shortcake in the whole wide world. No more chicken feed for me!"

"Yes sirree—just like Great-Granny, I'll be a cook! COOK-A-DOODLE-DO-O-O!" crowed Rooster as he pranced toward the big farmhouse.

FCAT Compare Characters

How is Rooster like Great-Granny? How is he different?

"*Cook*-a-doodle-doo?" said Dog.

"Have you lost your marbles, Rooster?" asked Cat.

"You've never cooked anything before!" said Goose.

"That doesn't matter," replied Rooster. "Cooking is in my blood—it's a family tradition. Now, who will help me?"

"Not I," said Dog.

"Not I," said Cat.

"Not I," said Goose.

And away they went.

Rooster pushed open the kitchen door. "It looks like I'm on my own … just like Great-Granny." He sighed and put on his apron.

"We'll help you."

Rooster turned, and there stood Turtle, Iguana, and Potbellied Pig.

"Do you three know anything about cooking?" Rooster asked.

"I can read recipes!" said Turtle.

"I can get stuff!" said Iguana.

"I can taste!" said Pig. "I'm an expert at tasting."

"Then we're a team," declared Rooster. "Let's get ready and start cooking!"

Turtle read the cookbook. "Heat oven to 450 degrees."

"I can do that!" said Iguana. "Look, I'll turn the knob. 150, 250, 350, 450. Hey, cooking is easy!"

Rooster put a big bowl on the table. "What's our first **ingredient**?" he asked.

"The recipe says we need flour," said Turtle.

"I can do that!" said Iguana. He dashed outside and picked a petunia. "How's this flower?"

Little Red Hen's Magnificent Strawberry Shortcake

A cookbook gives directions for making many different things to eat. Each type of food has its own recipe—a list of everything that goes into it and step-by-step directions on how to make it.

One of the oven knobs controls the temperature of the oven. The higher the number on the knob, the hotter the oven. Temperature is measured in degrees Fahrenheit (°F) or degrees Celsius (°C). On a very hot day the temperature outside can be over 100°F (38°C). Can you imagine what 450°F (232°C) feels like?

Ingredients are the different things that go into a recipe. Each ingredient may not taste good by itself, but if you put them all together in the right way, the result tastes delicious.

"No, no, no," said Rooster. "Not *that* kind of flower. We need flour for *cooking*. You know, the fluffy white stuff that's made from wheat."

"Can I taste the flour?" asked Pig.

"Not yet, Pig," said Turtle. "The recipe says to sift it first."

"What does *sift* mean?" asked Iguana.

"Hmmm," said Turtle. "I think *sift* means 'to search through' . . . "

Make sure you use a big bowl that will hold all of the ingredients. It's best to set out everything before you start cooking, so you don't have to go looking for your ingredients one-by-one like Iguana!

Flour is made from wheat grains that are finely ground. Long ago, the grinding was done by hand; now it is done by machines. Rooster's Great-Granny had to grind the grain into flour by hand, but you and Rooster can buy flour at the grocery store.

You will find many different kinds of flour at the store— including all-purpose flour, whole-wheat flour, cake flour, and high-altitude flour. Rooster's recipe calls for all-purpose flour.

Sifting adds air to the flour so it can be measured accurately. Some sifters have cranks, some have spring-action handles, and some are battery powered.

Make sure you put waxed paper on the counter before you start sifting. It will make cleanup a lot easier!

"You mean like when I sift through the garbage looking for lunch?" asked Pig.

"I can do that!" said Iguana. And he dived into the flour, throwing it everywhere!

"No, no, no," said Rooster. "Don't sift the flour like that. Put it through this sifter." Rooster turned the crank and sifted the flour into a big pile.

"Can I taste the pile?" asked Pig.

"Not yet, Pig," said Turtle. "Now we measure the flour."

"I can do that!" said Iguana. He grabbed a ruler. "The flour is four inches tall."

"No, no, no," said Rooster. "We don't want to know how *tall* it is. We want to know how *much* there is. We measure the flour with this metal measuring cup."

"We need two cups," added Turtle. "So fill it twice."

Rooster dumped the two cups of flour into the bowl.

"Can I taste it *now*?" asked Pig.

"Not yet, Pig," said Turtle. "Next we add two tablespoons of sugar, one tablespoon of baking powder, and one-half teaspoon of salt."

FCAT **Compare Characters**
How is Pig different from Rooster?

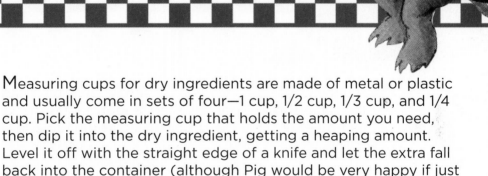

Measuring cups for dry ingredients are made of metal or plastic and usually come in sets of four—1 cup, 1/2 cup, 1/3 cup, and 1/4 cup. Pick the measuring cup that holds the amount you need, then dip it into the dry ingredient, getting a heaping amount. Level it off with the straight edge of a knife and let the extra fall back into the container (although Pig would be very happy if just a little fell on the floor!).

Dry ingredients can be measured in cups or grams.

1 cup = 227 grams

2 cups = 454 grams

Some ingredients are included for flavor, but not baking powder. Even Pig thinks it tastes terrible! When baking powder is added to the shortcake, bubbles of gas form and get bigger while the cake bakes, which makes it rise.

Dry ingredients are all sifted together so they will be evenly mixed.

"I can do that!" said Iguana. He looked under the table. "But where are the tablespoons?" He looked in the teapot. "No teaspoons in here!"

"No, no, no," said Rooster. "Don't look in the teapot or under the table! These spoons are for measuring. Each holds a certain amount." Rooster measured the sugar, baking powder, and salt, poured them into the big bowl, then sifted all the dry ingredients together.

Iguana wasn't far off when he looked for tablespoons under the table and teaspoons in the teapot. Tablespoons were named after the large spoons used at the table to serve soup, and teaspoons after the smaller spoons used to stir tea.

3 teaspoons = 1 tablespoon = 14 grams

Butter is made by churning cream, the fat in cow's milk. (This doesn't mean it comes from a fat cow!) Margarine can be used instead of butter. Butter and margarine come in sticks and are easy to measure because their wrappers are marked in tablespoons.

1 stick butter = 1/2 cup = 8 tablespoons = 113 grams

Butter and margarine are two types of solid shortening, or fat, used in cooking. The name "shortcake" doesn't mean the cake is short—it refers to the shortening in the recipe.

Cool butter is "cut in" to dry ingredients by using two table knives or a pastry blender. Cut the butter into tiny pieces.

"Looks awfully white in there," said Pig. "I better taste it."

"Not yet, Pig," said Turtle. "Now we add butter. We need one stick."

"I can do that!" cried Iguana. He raced outside and broke off a branch. "How's this stick?"

"No, no, no," said Rooster. "Not *that* kind of stick. A stick of *butter*." Rooster unwrapped the butter and dropped it into the bowl.

"That butter is just sitting there like a log," said Pig. "Maybe I need to taste it."

"Not yet, Pig," said Turtle. "Next we cut in the butter."

"I can do that!" said Iguana. "Uh-oh. Scissors don't cut butter very well."

"No, no, no," said Rooster. "Don't cut the butter with scissors. Use these two table knives, like this."

Rooster cut in the butter until the mixture was crumbly.

"Looks mighty dry in there," said Pig. "Perhaps I should taste it."

"Not yet, Pig," said Turtle. "Now the recipe says to beat one egg."

"I can do that!" cried Iguana.

"No, no, no," said Rooster. "Don't beat an egg with a baseball bat! We use an eggbeater." Rooster carefully broke the egg into a dish, beat it with the eggbeater, and poured it into the big bowl.

"That looks tasty," said Pig. "Please let me taste it."

"Not yet, Pig," said Turtle. "Now add milk. We need two-thirds of a cup."

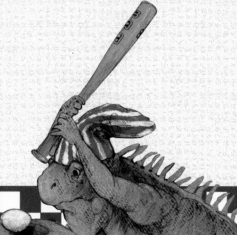

Break an egg by hitting the shell gently on the edge of a countertop or bowl to make a small crack. Place both thumbs in the crack and pull the shell apart. Always crack an egg into a small bowl before you add it to the other ingredients in case the egg is bad or shell pieces fall in. Eggs add color and flavor and help hold the cake together.

You can beat eggs with a fork, a hand beater (like Rooster's), or an electric mixer. If you use an electric mixer, make sure to put the eggs in a big bowl and start off on a low speed. If you start with the mixer on high, you'll get egg on your face!

Liquid measuring cups are made of glass or plastic. Each measuring cup has a spout for pouring and extra room below the rim so you don't have to fill it to the top and worry about spilling. Always put the cup on a flat surface and measure at eye level.

Grease the pan with a solid shortening so the cake will not stick.

Rooster is mixing the batter by hand, which means to stir with a spoon instead of a mixer. (How would Iguana mix by hand?)

"I can do that!" said Iguana. "Here, hold that glass measuring cup and I'll saw off a third. We'll use the other two-thirds to measure the milk."

"Wait," said Pig. "Why don't we fill the measuring cup to the top and I'll drink down a third?"

"No, no, no," said Rooster. "The cup has marks on it—1/3—2/3—1 cup. We'll fill it to the 2/3 mark." Rooster poured the milk into the bowl.

"It surely needs tasting now!" said Pig.

"Not yet, Pig," said Turtle. "Now we mix the dough and put it in a greased baking pan." Rooster stirred and spread as Turtle read, "Bake in the oven for fifteen to eighteen minutes."

"I can do that!" cried Iguana.

Iguana shoved the pan into the oven. "Let's see, fifteen minutes equals nine hundred seconds. I'll count them. One, two, three, four—"

"No, no, no," said Rooster, and he set the timer so that Iguana would stop counting the seconds. Pig burned his tongue on the oven door trying to taste the shortcake. Turtle studied the cookbook to see what to do next.

"Let's cut up the strawberries and whip the cream," said Turtle.

Make sure you stay nearby, so you can hear the timer when your cake is ready! Cooking times are given in hours, minutes, or seconds.
1 hour = 60 minutes
1 minute = 60 seconds

Wash the strawberries first and cut off their tops. Use a cutting board and cut each strawberry in half, then cut each half in half. (How many pieces do you have now?) Watch out for your fingers!

Whipping cream comes from cow's milk. It contains more butterfat than regular cream. Iguana might think you use a whip to whip the cream, but you could use an eggbeater or electric mixer.

When you take something out of a hot oven, make sure you use a pot holder or oven mitt.

A trick to tell if your shortcake is done: Stick a toothpick or knife in the center of the cake. If it comes out clean, without any cake sticking to it, the shortcake is ready.

Don't forget to turn off the oven when you're finished!

And they cut and cut and whipped and whipped, until
… *ding!*

Rooster grabbed the oven mitt off Iguana's head and
took the shortcake carefully out of the oven.

"Oh, it's beautiful, and it smells *sooo* good," said Pig.
"I know I have to taste it now."

"Not yet, Pig," said Turtle. "We need to let it cool."

Soon the shortcake was ready to cut. Rooster sliced
it in half.

They stacked one layer of cake, one layer of whipped cream, one layer of strawberries.

Then again—cake, cream, berries.

It looked just like the picture of the strawberry shortcake in the cookbook.

"This is the most wonderful, magnificent strawberry shortcake in the whole wide world," said Rooster. "If Great-Granny could see me now! Let's take it to the table."

"I can do that!" cried Iguana.

He yanked at the plate. The shortcake tilted … and slid …

splat!

Right on the floor.

Pig was ready. "Now it's my turn—to taste it!"

In a split second the strawberry shortcake was gone. Every last crumb had disappeared into the potbelly of the pig.

"Our shortcake!" Iguana cried. "You ate it!"

"I thought it was my turn," replied Pig. "I'm the taster, remember? And it tasted great!"

"But it was our **masterpiece**," moaned Turtle.

"And a **tasty** one, too," said Pig. "Now we can make something else."

"Yeah …" Iguana glared. "How about a plump, juicy roast pig?"

Pig gasped. "Roast pig? How about iguana potpie—or—or—turtle soup!"

"No, no, no!" cried Rooster. "Listen to me! We made this shortcake as a team, and teams work together."

"But Pig ate it!" whined Turtle.

"Iguana dropped it," pouted Pig.

"Turtle should have caught it," grumbled Iguana.

"It doesn't matter," said Rooster. "The first shortcake was just for practice. It won't be as hard to make the second time!"

"Well," added Turtle, "we don't have to worry about messing up the kitchen. It's already a mess."

"So, who will help me make it again?" asked Rooster.

Pig, Turtle, and Iguana looked at each other.

"I will!" said Pig.

"I will!" said Turtle.

"I will!" said Iguana.

"Cook-a-doodle-dooooo!" crowed Rooster. "Let's get cooking again!"

Together they made the second most wonderful, magnificent strawberry shortcake in the whole wide world. And it was a lot easier than the first time!

What's Cookin' With Janet and Susan?

Janet Stevens and Susan Stevens Crummel

Authors **Janet Stevens** and **Susan Stevens Crummel** were not very close when they were growing up, but now they have as much fun working together as the animals in their story did.

They are sisters who both like animals. Janet's favorite books as a child were about animals. She still reads animal stories today. Janet likes telling old tales in new ways, just as she did in this story. The sisters wrote this book together. Then Janet created the illustrations. She's been drawing ever since she was a child.

Other books by Janet Stevens and Susan Stevens Crummel: *Jackalope* and *And the Dish Ran Away with the Spoon*

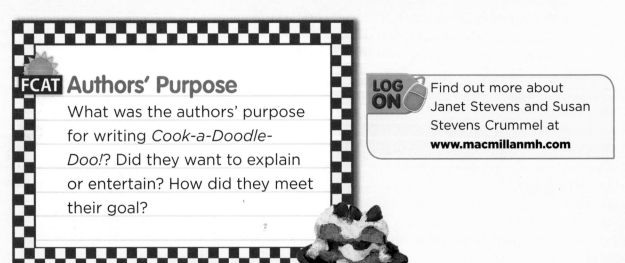

FCAT Authors' Purpose

What was the authors' purpose for writing *Cook-a-Doodle-Doo!*? Did they want to explain or entertain? How did they meet their goal?

LOG ON Find out more about Janet Stevens and Susan Stevens Crummel at **www.macmillanmh.com**

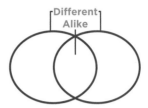 **FCAT** Comprehension Check

Summarize

Summarize *Cook-a-Doodle-Doo!* Use the Venn Diagram to help you compare Pig and Rooster. Compare and contrast the main characters. Use descriptions of their personalities and events in the story.

Think and Compare

1. How does Rooster change from the beginning to the end of the story? Use details from the story in your answer. **Make Inferences and Analyze: Compare Characters**

2. Which character is most helpful to Rooster? Which character is least helpful? Explain why. Support your answer with information from the story. **Analyze**

3. Suppose you wanted to bake a cake. Which of the characters in the story would you ask to help you? Why? **Apply**

4. Why is it important to follow directions in **recipes**? Explain your answer. **Evaluate**

5. Read "Red and Her Friends" on pages 12–13. How is it similar to *Cook-a-Doodle-Doo!*? How are the two stories different? Use details from both stories in your answer. **Reading/Writing Across Texts**

Science

Genre

Nonfiction Articles give facts about persons, places, or things.

FCAT Text Feature

Diagrams are drawings that help you understand information in the text.

Content Vocabulary

measurements

temperature

thermometer

WELCOME TO THE BAKERY!

By Jin Lee

Items on a bakery shelf are fun to look at. They smell great. They are tasty. Did you know that baking is serious business? One wrong step and your favorite bread could turn into mush. Or it could turn into a heavy rock!

The Science of Baking

Bakers must follow recipes and measure ingredients to make sure that they use the exact amounts. Bakers also must mix ingredients in the right order.

Take a good look at a slice of bread. What do you notice? Bread is light. It is filled with little air holes. To make bread light and fluffy, a baker measures carefully. Too much salt can ruin the loaf. Too little salt can ruin it, too!

Cups and Spoons

To make bread, the baker mixes milk, sugar, salt, shortening, flour, and yeast. Yeast is the ingredient that makes the bread rise. Special cups and spoons with just the right space for each ingredient are used. Spoons and cups can be used to measure the dry ingredients. Spoon **measurements** can be as small as 1/8 of a teaspoon or as large as a tablespoon.

Another measuring tool a baker uses is a cup—but not the cup you drink from! There are special containers that hold cup measurements, such as 1/4 cup and 2 cups. Only exact measurements will do when baking.

Hot and Cold

The **temperature** of the water used to dissolve the yeast must also be measured. To measure water temperature, a baker uses a **thermometer**. The temperature of a bread mixture will change as new ingredients are added. If the ingredients are too hot or too cold, the bread will not bake properly.

The baker must take the bread out of the oven at exactly the right time.

The Right Stuff

Bread dough should be sticky. This happens when the right amounts of water and flour are used. If the baker uses too much flour, it will soak up all the water. If there is too much water in the bowl, the dough will be too watery. Each ingredient must be exact, or the bread will not look right. It may not have good **flavor**, or taste.

HOW BREAD IS MADE

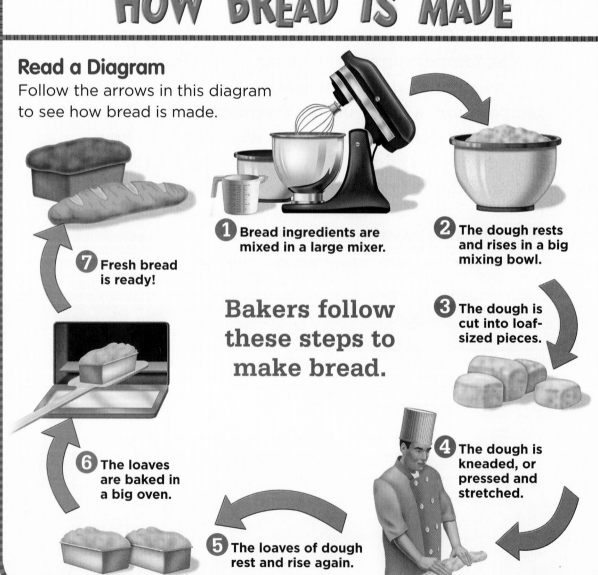

Read a Diagram
Follow the arrows in this diagram to see how bread is made.

Bakers follow these steps to make bread.

1 Bread ingredients are mixed in a large mixer.

2 The dough rests and rises in a big mixing bowl.

3 The dough is cut into loaf-sized pieces.

4 The dough is kneaded, or pressed and stretched.

5 The loaves of dough rest and rise again.

6 The loaves are baked in a big oven.

7 Fresh bread is ready!

If you have a favorite recipe, make sure you follow it exactly. Measure each ingredient carefully. The baker knows how important correct measurement is. Remember to think like a baker next time you follow a recipe.

TABLE OF MEASUREMENTS

Volume of Fluids	
8 fluid ounces (fl oz)	1 cup (c)
2 cups	1 pint (pt)
2 pints	1 quart (qt)
4 quarts	1 gallon (gal)
Weight	
16 ounces (oz)	1 pound (lb)

FCAT **Connect and Compare**

1. Look at the diagram called How Bread Is Made. What happens first? What happens last? **Reading a Diagram**

2. Why is it so important to measure carefully when making bread? **Explain**

3. How is making bread like making a strawberry shortcake in *Cook-A-Doodle-Do*? **Reading/Writing Across Texts**

 Science Activity

Find a recipe for something you like to eat. Draw a diagram that shows the steps you take to make it.

LOG ON Find out more about baking at
www.macmillanmh.com

Writer's Craft

FCAT Vary Sentences

Good writers **vary** the types of **sentences** they use. They also vary the lengths of their sentences.

Write About a Family Meal

I began my story with a question and an exclamation.

I used long and short sentences to give my writing variety.

Breakfast Surprise

by Marcus G.

What tasty treat is shaped like an animal? Pancakes! Last weekend Dad taught us how to make animal pancakes for breakfast. First we helped him mix the ingredients in a bowl. I was in charge of the salt and sugar. My brothers were in charge of the flour. They made a big mess! "We must clean as we go along," Dad warned. Dad poured the mixture onto the hot griddle and asked us to name our favorite animals. Before we knew it, we had animal pancakes!

My brother asked, "Can I have a walrus?" Dad tried to make one, but it looked like a rabbit to me! It was the best breakfast. Pancakes are now my favorite food!

Writing Prompt

Families sometimes like to make things together.

Think of something you have made with your family.

Now write a story about what you made with your family.

FCAT Writer's Checklist

✓ **Focus:** I have a clear topic.

✓ **Organization:** I tell the story in the order in which it happened.

✓ **Support:** I include specific details that support my main idea.

☐ **Conventions:** I use the verbs *be, do,* and *have* correctly. I **vary** my **sentences.** All my words are spelled correctly.

Getting Along

Talk About It

People can have different ideas and still work together. What do you do when someone disagrees with you?

LOG ON Find out more about getting along at **www.macmillanmh.com**

Community Works

by Jenna Rabin

One bright day, as the sunlight **beamed** through the windows, Mr. Turner's class started to plan the third-grade community service project.

"Okay," said Mr. Turner. "Let's share some ideas and listen to each other."

A few students raised their hands. Mr. Turner called on Mark. "We could clean up the small park—pick up trash and paint the benches," said Mark.

Rachel got annoyed. She **argued** with Mark. "You just want that park clean for yourself. Everyone else uses the big park across town. I think we should serve meals at the homeless shelter."

"Now, Rachel. Everyone should have a chance to share his or her ideas. It's okay to disagree, but we should still treat each other nicely."

"Sorry, Mr. Turner," Rachel said.

Jen cut in, "There are people who don't have many **possessions**, not even warm clothing. We could collect **fabric** for making nice, warm clothes for them!"

Cara added, "I read about a class that raised money and **purchased** notebooks and pencils for kids from a discount store."

"We could do crafts with people in nursing homes or hospitals," said Maria.

"Crafts?" groaned Sameer. "I'm really bad at crafts. I'm all thumbs! But how about a walkathon. I'm a fast walker, and we'd get exercise," he said. This made everyone laugh and stop their **quarreling** over who had the best idea.

Then Mr. Turner spoke. "All of your ideas are great. I'm going to write them on the board. Then we will take a class vote. This way we can choose a community service project that most people want to do."

The students agreed this was a good plan.

Reread for **Comprehension**

Make Inferences and Analyze

FCAT **Plot Development** Authors sometimes give readers **clues** about characters, setting, and story events. Readers should analyze these clues and **draw conclusions**. You can draw a conclusion about the characters, setting, or events by using story clues and what you already know. Reread the selection. Use your Conclusion Map to draw a conclusion about Rachel. Use Rachel's actions and reactions as your clues.

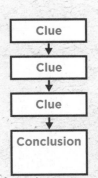

Comprehension

Genre

A **Fable** is a short story that teaches a moral.

Make Inferences and Analyze

Plot Development

As you read, use your Conclusion Map.

Clue

↓

Clue

↓

Clue

↓

Conclusion

Read to Find Out

How will the brothers get along at the end of the story?

50

Seven Spools of Thread

A KWANZAA STORY

BY **ANGELA SHELF MEDEARIS**

ILLUSTRATED BY **DANIEL MINTER**

Award
Winning
Selection

51

In a small African village in the country of Ghana there lived an old man and his seven sons. After the death of his wife, the old man became both father and mother to the boys. The seven brothers were handsome young men. Their skin was as smooth and dark as the finest mahogany wood. Their limbs were as straight and strong as warriors' spears.

But they were a disappointment to their father. From morning until night, the family's small home was filled with the sound of the brothers' **quarreling**.

As soon as the sun brought forth a new day, the brothers began to argue. They **argued** all morning about how to tend the crops. They argued all afternoon about the weather.

"It is hot," said the middle son.

"No—a cool breeze is blowing!" said the second son.

They argued all evening about when to return home.

"It will be dark soon," the youngest said. "Let's finish this row and begin anew tomorrow."

"No, it's too early to stop," called the third son.

"Can't you see the sun is setting?" shouted the sixth son.

And so it would continue until the moon **beamed** down and the stars twinkled in the sky.

54

At mealtime, the young men argued until the stew was cold and the fu fu was hard.

"You gave him more than you gave me," whined the third son.

"I divided the food equally," said their father.

"I will starve with only this small portion on my plate," complained the youngest.

"If you don't want it, I'll eat it!" said the oldest son. He grabbed a handful of meat from his brother's plate.

"Stop being so greedy!" said the youngest.

And so it went on every night. It was often morning before the seven brothers finished dinner.

One sad day, the old man died and was buried. At sunrise the next morning, the village Chief called the brothers before him.

"Your father has left an inheritance," said the Chief.

The brothers whispered excitedly among themselves.

"I know my father left me everything because I am the oldest son," said the oldest.

"I know my father left me everything because I am the youngest son," said the youngest.

"He left everything to me," said the middle son. "I know I was his favorite."

"Eeeh!" said the second son. "Everything is mine!"

The brothers began shouting and shoving. Soon, all seven were rolling around on the ground, hitting and kicking each other.

"Stop that this instant!" the Chief shouted.

The brothers stopped fighting. They shook the dust off their clothes and sat before the Chief, eyeing each other suspiciously.

"Your father has decreed that all of his property and **possessions** will be divided among you equally," said the Chief. "But first, by the time the moon rises tonight, you must learn how to make gold out of these spools of silk thread. If you do not, you will be turned out of your home as beggars."

The oldest brother received blue thread. The next brother, red. The next, yellow. The middle son was given orange thread; the next, green; the next, black; and the youngest son received white thread. For once, the brothers were speechless.

The Chief spoke again. "From this moment forward, you must not argue among yourselves or raise your hands in anger towards one another. If you do, your father's property and all his possessions will be divided equally among the poorest of the villagers. Go quickly; you only have a little time."

The brothers bowed to the Chief and hurried away.

FCAT Plot Development
Why were the brothers speechless after listening to the Chief?

57

When the seven Ashanti brothers arrived at their farm, something unusual happened. They sat side by side, from the oldest to the youngest, without saying anything unkind to each other.

"My brothers," the oldest said after a while, "let us shake hands and make peace among ourselves."

"Let us never argue or fight again," said the youngest brother.

The brothers placed their hands together and held each other tightly.

For the first time in years, peace rested within the walls of their home.

"My brothers," said the third son quietly, "surely our father would not turn us into the world as beggars."

"I agree," said the middle son. "I do not believe our father would have given us the task of turning thread into gold if it were impossible."

"Could it be," said the oldest son, "that there might be small pieces of gold in this thread?"

The sun beamed hotly overhead. Yellow streams of light crept inside the hut. Each brother held up his spool of thread. The beautiful colors sparkled in the sunlight. But there were no nuggets of gold in these spools.

"I'm afraid not, my brother," said the sixth son. "But that was a good idea."

"Thank you, my brother," said the oldest.

"Could it be," said the youngest, "that by making something from this thread we could earn a fortune in gold?"

"Perhaps," said the oldest, "we could make cloth out of this thread and sell it. I believe we can do it."

"This is a good plan," said the middle son. "But we do not have enough of any one color to make a full bolt of cloth."

"What if," said the third son, "we weave the thread together to make a cloth of many colors?"

"But our people do not wear cloth like that," said the fifth son. "We wear only cloth of one color."

"Maybe," said the second, "we could make a cloth that is so special, everyone will want to wear it."

"My brothers," said the sixth son, "we could finish faster if we all worked together."

"I know we can succeed," said the middle son.

The seven Ashanti brothers went to work. Together they cut the wood to make a loom. The younger brothers held the pieces together while the older brothers assembled the loom.

They took turns weaving cloth out of their spools of thread. They made a pattern of stripes and shapes that looked like the wings of birds. They used all the colors—blue, red, yellow, orange, green, black, and white. Soon the brothers had several pieces of beautiful multicolored cloth.

When the cloth was finished, the seven brothers took turns neatly folding the brightly colored **fabric**. Then they placed it into seven baskets and put the baskets on their heads.

The brothers formed a line from the oldest to the youngest and began the journey to the village. The sun slowly made a golden path across the sky. The brothers hurried down the long, dusty road as quickly as they could.

As soon as they entered the marketplace, the seven Ashanti brothers called out, "Come and buy the most wonderful cloth in the world! Come and buy the most wonderful cloth in the world!"

They unfolded a bolt and held it up for all to see. The multicolored fabric glistened like a rainbow. A crowd gathered around the seven Ashanti brothers.

"Oh," said one villager. "I have never seen cloth so beautiful! Look at the unusual pattern!"

"Ah," said another. "This is the finest fabric in all the land! Feel the texture!"

FCAT Plot Development
What have the brothers learned?

The brothers smiled proudly. Suddenly, a man dressed in magnificent robes pushed his way to the front of the crowd. Everyone stepped back respectfully. It was the King's treasurer. He rubbed the cloth between the palms of his hands. Then he held it up to the sunlight.

"What a thing of beauty," he said, fingering the material. "This cloth will make a wonderful gift for the King! I must have all of it."

The seven brothers whispered together.

"Cloth fit for a king," said the oldest, "should be **purchased** at a price only a king can pay. It is yours for one bag of gold."

"Sold," said the King's treasurer. He untied his bag of gold and spilled out many pieces for the brothers.

The seven Ashanti brothers ran out of the marketplace and back down the road to their village.

A shining silver moon began to creep up in the sky. Panting and dripping with sweat, the brothers threw themselves before the Chief's hut.

"Oh, Chief," said the oldest, "we have turned the thread into gold!"

The Chief came out of his hut and sat upon a stool.

The oldest brother poured the gold out onto the ground.

"Have you argued or fought today?" asked the Chief.

"No, my Chief," said the youngest. "We have been too busy working together to argue or fight."

"Then you have learned the lesson your father sought to teach you," said the Chief. "All that he had is now yours."

The older brothers smiled happily, but the youngest son looked sad.

"What about the poor people in the village?" he asked. "We receive an inheritance, but what will they do?"

"Perhaps," said the oldest, "we can teach them how to turn thread into gold."

The Chief smiled. "You have learned your lesson very well."

The seven Ashanti brothers taught their people carefully. The village became famous for its beautiful, multicolored cloth, and the villagers prospered.

From that day until this, the seven Ashanti brothers have worked together, farming the land.

And they have worked peacefully, in honor of their father.

Sticks in a bundle are unbreakable.

—*African Proverb*

71

WEAVING A TALE WITH ANGELA AND DANIEL

Author **Angela Shelf Medearis** wrote this story to celebrate the African American holiday Kwanzaa. When Angela was growing up, there were no books for her to read about her African American heritage. Today she writes books about African Americans so readers can feel proud of who they are.

Illustrator **Daniel Minter** often carves and paints on wood, just as he did for this story. Woodcarving is an important part of traditional African art. Daniel's carvings help keep these traditional arts alive.

Other books by Angela Shelf Medearis: *Too Much Talk* and *The Freedom Riddle*

 LOG ON Find out more about Angela Shelf Medearis and Daniel Minter at **www.macmillanmh.com**

FCAT Author's Purpose

Did Angela Shelf Medearis write this story to explain, inform, or entertain? What clues tell you her purpose for writing?

FCAT Comprehension Check

Summarize

Summarize the plot of *Seven Spools of Thread.* Use your Conclusion Map to help you recall clues that tell how the brothers behave at the end.

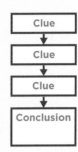

Clue
↓
Clue
↓
Clue
↓
Conclusion

Think and Compare

1. Why does the Chief order the brothers to make gold from thread? How is this different from ordering them to stop **quarreling**? Use details from the story to support your answer. **Make Inferences and Analyze: Plot Development**

2. Look back at pages 61–63. What lesson about teamwork do the brothers learn? Use story details in your answer. **Analyze**

3. Think of a time you had to work with a friend or family member. What did you learn from your experience? **Apply**

4. The brothers teach the villagers how to weave the special cloth. Why is this better than giving the villagers money? Explain. **Evaluate**

5. Reread "Community Works" on pages 48–49. How is the problem in that story similar to the problem in *Seven Spools of Thread*? How are the solutions to the problems different? Use details from both stories in your answer. **Reading/ Writing Across Texts**

WHAT CAUSES DAY AND NIGHT?

by Keisha Oliver

Believe it or not, people used to think that Earth stood still while the sun traveled around it each day. It is simple to see why they thought this. The sun rises in the morning, moves across the sky, and disappears at night. Today we know much more about the movement of Sun and Earth.

The movement of Earth causes day and night. Earth is shaped like a ball, or **sphere**. As Earth **rotates**, or turns, there is daylight where Earth faces the sun. There is darkness where Earth is turned away from the sun.

Earth is rotating all the time, but we do not feel it. It takes 24 hours for Earth to make one full rotation. This rotation is equal to one day.

RULES FOR DAYTIME AND NIGHTTIME

Reading Rules

Follow these rules to help you stay safe when you are outside in the daytime or the nighttime.

Daytime Rules

1. Do not look directly at the sun.
2. Wear sunglasses when outside in daylight.
3. Wear sunscreen.

Nighttime Rules

1. Wear bright clothing so you can be seen.
2. Make sure you tell a responsible adult where you are at all times.

74

EARTH MOVES!

Earth rotates around an imaginary line called an **axis**. The axis is drawn through the center of Earth. The equator is a name for the imaginary circle that goes around the middle of Earth.

Since Earth is tilted toward or away from the sun, the amount of heat and energy changes at different places. The temperature is warmer at the equator and colder at the two poles. Earth's tilt also changes the amount of light found in different places at different times of the year. This is why night can last for months in Alaska!

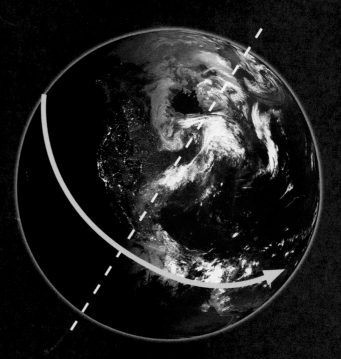

As Earth moves around the sun, it turns on its axis. Places near the equator receive nearly the same amount of sunlight all year long.

 FCAT **Connect and Compare**

1. Look at the diagram above. Describe Earth's axis. **Reading a Diagram**

2. How long does it take Earth to make a complete rotation? Describe how this rotation affects daylight. **Recall**

3. Why is the sun important in *Seven Spools of Thread*? **Reading Across Texts**

Science Activity

Research two areas of Earth with different temperatures. Write a paragraph summarizing your research. Draw a diagram to explain how the tilt of Earth on its axis affects the temperatures in the areas you researched.

 Find out more about day and night at **www.macmillanmh.com**

Writer's Craft

FCAT **Precise Words**

A writer uses **precise words** to make the meaning clear. Precise words make writing easy to understand. This is especially important when writing instructions.

I choose a precise word to describe the place mat.

I use precise verbs to tell the reader what to do.

Make a Rainbow Place Mat

by Peter K.

A rainbow-colored place mat is easy to make. You will need tape, scissors, and paper in several colors.

1. Fold a piece of paper in half.
2. Starting from the fold, make five cuts that end one inch from the paper's edge. Unfold.
3. Cut one-inch-wide strips from the other pieces of paper. Then weave the strips between the cuts you made.
4. Tape the strips in place. Pound them lightly to make them stick.
5. Your place mat is ready to use!

Writing Prompt

People write directions to tell how to do something.

Think about something you know how to do.

Now write directions to explain how to do something.

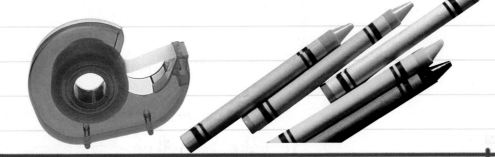

 FCAT Writer's Checklist

 Focus: I choose a topic and identify my purpose—to explain.

 Organization: My directions present the steps in order. I use numbers to show the order.

Support: I choose **precise words** that make the meaning clear.

 Conventions: I use linking verbs correctly. I use the correct punctuation at the end of complete sentences.

Talk About It

Why do people need the natural resources shown on these pages?

 Find out more about natural resources at **www.macmillanmh.com**

Protecting Our Natural Resources

Vocabulary

native
shouldn't
research
sprout
clumps

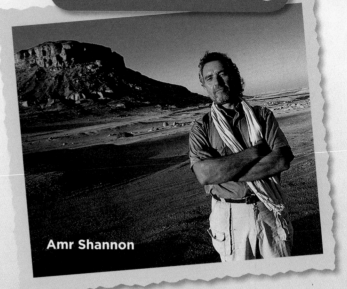

Amr Shannon

Saving Egypt's Great Desert

Egypt's vast Western Desert is 600 miles long and 900 miles wide—and it's very hot. Temperatures in the summer can go up to 100 degrees.

The Western Desert used to be one of Earth's most private spots, but now it is different. Many visitors are making it a popular tourist attraction. New roads and buildings are threatening **native** plants and animals of the desert ecosystem. Some visitors even remove priceless fossils from the desert.

Amr (AH•muhr) Shannon is an expert on the Western Desert. He wants to protect it, especially an area known as the Valley of the Whales. It is full of ancient crocodile, shark, and whale fossils.

"Fossils are disappearing at a very fast rate," says Shannon. They **shouldn't** be removed.

Shannon thinks kids between the ages of 6 and 12 can learn to protect the desert. He takes groups of kids on a two-day desert adventure for hands-on **research**. "I find that children absorb more than adults," he says. "They are the future, the ones who are really going to make a difference."

An ancient crocodile fossil from the Valley of the Whales

Earth's Biomes

A biome is a large community of plants and animals that live in a certain type of climate. Here's a look at the seven major biomes in the world.

Polar Bear

Arctic Tundra
A cold area in the far north around the Arctic Ocean. The frozen soil makes it impossible for trees to **sprout**, or grow, from seed. It is Earth's coldest biome.

Orchid

Rain Forest
A wet and humid forest that receives at least 70 inches of rain a year. **Clumps**—groups growing close together—of mosses and fungi grow on the forest floor.

Cactus

Desert
A dry area that gets very little rainfall. There are two kinds of deserts: hot and dry, or cold and dry.

Mountains
Very cold and windy environments that exist on every continent.

Mountain Goat

Deciduous Forest
Found in mild-temperature zones. It is mostly made up of trees that lose their leaves.

Raccoon

Grasslands
Vast areas of grassy fields, perfect for growing food.

Zebra

Coniferous Forest
A biome of cone-bearing trees south of the Arctic tundra.

Snowshoe Hare

Dana Beach

Sandy Island's Best Beach

Kids who live on Sandy Island in South Carolina ride to their classes on a school boat! The island has rare trees, birds, plants, and only 120 people.

When some landowners wanted to build a bridge to the mainland, the islanders feared it would ruin the natural environment. Environmentalist Dana Beach and other islanders stopped the bridge. Then he helped turn the endangered longleaf-pine forest into a nature preserve to protect it forever.

LOG ON Find out more about nature preserves at www.macmillanmh.com

WASHINGTON WEED WHACKERS

WHAT ALIEN SPECIES IS CREEPING ALONG THE SHORES OF PUGET SOUND?

The "weed whackers" of Lincoln Elementary, in Mount Vernon, Washington

Spartina is a perfectly good plant. It creates a habitat and food for many fish and wildlife. So why do the kids at Lincoln Elementary School in Mount Vernon, Washington, want to get rid of it? It's because spartina **shouldn't** live on the West Coast. In Washington State's Puget Sound, spartina has turned into a life-choking weed.

Spartina is **native** to the East Coast. There, native plants and animals keep it from growing out of control. Besides providing a wetland habitat, spartina's roots stop soil from being washed away. In Washington, however, spartina is a different kind of plant. Its traits are not helpful. Spartina is an alien species since it does not grow there naturally.

AN ALIEN ATTACKS!

Since no animals eat spartina in Puget Sound, it grows in thick **clumps**, crowding out native plants. Its roots hurt rather than help. "It clogs up all the mud and changes the shape of the mud flats," explains student Seth Morris. In the East it creates a good habitat, but in the West, it has caused crabs, snails, salmon, and shorebirds to leave because there is less food.

This photo shows how spartina is spreading in Puget Sound and has crowded out native plants. Spartina is easy to dig up when it's young, but after a couple of years, it grows deep, thick roots and is very hard to remove.

When the kids at Lincoln Elementary School took on the spartina problem, they didn't know how the plant got to the Northwest. The kids contacted local experts and hit the books to do some **research**.

WHERE DID IT COME FROM?

Students Seth Morris and Anna Hansen reported that spartina came to Puget Sound in a few ways. "Spartina goes back to the late 1800s, when it came here from the East Coast," Seth explains. Settlers wanted to raise oysters in the West. They packed them in wet spartina to keep them fresh. When the oysters were put in new beds in Puget Sound, it made spartina seeds **sprout**.

Spartina was also introduced when duck hunters planted it to attract more ducks. Engineers brought the plant in to keep soil from washing away, and farmers planted it to feed their cattle.

TAKING ACTION

The classes worked in teams. One team researched Padilla Bay. Another team made drawings of spartina and its effects on the shore. The third team worked to get the word out about spartina. All the kids wrote letters to state lawmakers, urging them to help.

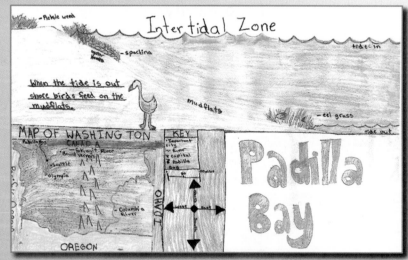

A student's drawing shows where spartina has invaded Padilla Bay.

Getting rid of spartina takes lots of hard work and money. That's why the students wanted to teach the community about the weed. First, they held town meetings to discuss spartina's impact on the environment. They also traveled to the state capitol in Olympia to talk about the problem. The kids even headed to Padilla Bay to snip off spartina seed heads to keep the weed from spreading.

"One of the big lessons we learned from this project," says their teacher, Teresa Vaughn, "was that we can't take care of the problem by just taking care of it in our bay. This is a problem for the entire Northwest coast."

The kids know that saving Padilla Bay will be hard work. It took decades for the spartina problem to take root. It'll take many years to get rid of it.

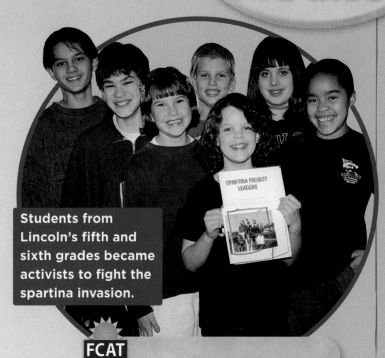

Students from Lincoln's fifth and sixth grades became activists to fight the spartina invasion.

FCAT
Think and Compare

1. What is the difference between spartina growth in the East and in Washington?

2. Why is spartina described as an alien?

3. Why is getting rid of spartina so difficult?

4. How have people caused the problems described in "Saving Egypt's Great Desert" and "Washington Weed Whackers"?

up a Creek

Steelhead trout are members of the rainbow trout family. They are common in the Pacific Ocean, Asia, and North America.

Students in Jean Mahoney's class worked all year to clean up Arana Creek in California. Arana Creek is part of the Arana Gulch watershed. A watershed is an area where water from rivers, creeks, rain, or snow drains into a larger body of water. The Arana Gulch watershed is a 3.5 square mile basin that includes the Arana Creek and the area around it.

Watersheds are perfect habitats for steelhead trout to lay eggs, but the Arana Gulch is polluted. The creek is clogged with sediment, or loose dirt, that falls into the bay and smothers fish eggs. Small amounts of sediment are natural and do not hurt the fish eggs. But recent storms have caused too much sediment to build up.

After Ms. Mahoney's class learned about the area's plants and animals, they went to work. They picked up trash and removed weeds. Then they planted trees and grasses to help hold the soil together. The new trees and grasses would keep the sediment from flowing into the creek. Trees also create shade which helps provide shelter for wildlife in the watershed.

After they helped control soil erosion, the students wanted to help the trout swim safely down the creek to the bay. They changed how the water flowed, making it easier for the fish to swim down the creek. The students cleared sandy areas that stuck out into the creek. These areas were stopping the steelhead trout from swimming easily.

The following spring they tested the water temperature and sediment levels. Conditions were just right for the trout. Today, the watershed is tested regularly. It is once again a good place for plants and animals to call home.

Go on ▶

1 How does pollution affect fish in a natural habitat?

(A) It creates a watershed to protect them.

(B) It decreases the average water temperature.

(C) It makes it hard for fish to swim and for their eggs to hatch.

(D) It reduces the amount of sediment.

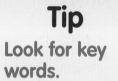

Tip
Look for key words.

2 How would you describe the students in Ms. Mahoney's class?

(F) excited about trout fishing

(G) tired of picking up trash and weeds

(H) interested in protecting the environment

(I) unhappy about working outside the classroom

3 Compare the Arana Creek before Ms. Mahoney's class cleaned it with the creek after the students helped.

(A) Before, the creek was part of the basin; after, it became part of a new watershed.

(B) Before, the creek was part of a man-made lake; after, it drained into the sea.

(C) Before, the creek was full of sediment; after, the water flowed easily.

(D) Before, the creek was 3.5 square miles; after, it was 4 miles long.

4 In what ways was Arana Creek better off after Jean Mahoney's class worked on it? Use details from the article in your answer.

5 What are some qualities of a good volunteer? How were the students in Ms. Mahoney's class good volunteers? Use information from the article in your answer.

Write to a Prompt

Sometimes people have amazing things happen to them.
Think about an amazing thing that could happen to you.
Now <u>write about</u> this amazing thing that could happen to you.

> Narrative writing tells a story about a personal or fictional experience.

> To figure out if a writing prompt asks for narrative writing, look for clue words, such as <u>write about</u>, <u>tell what happened</u>, and <u>write a story</u>.

Below see how one student begins a response to the prompt above.

The beginning of the story explains the setting, or where the story takes place.

→ Today was the big day! I had volunteered to talk about our school fundraising project on TV. I entered the studio ready for my big TV break.

Soon, we went on live. First, I answered questions. Then I said, "We need to educate people about the needs of others in their communities. Local shelters should be well-stocked for emergencies. This takes time and money."

Then the host said, "We have someone here who can help you with that."

Suddenly, the President of the United States walked onto the stage. "I think I can help," he said. The President handed me a check for two million dollars!

Writing Prompt

Respond in writing to the prompt below. Before you write, read the Writing Hints for Prompts. Remember to review the hints after you finish writing.

FCAT People sometimes have unusual days.

Think about how a day could be unusual.

Now write a story about an unusual day.

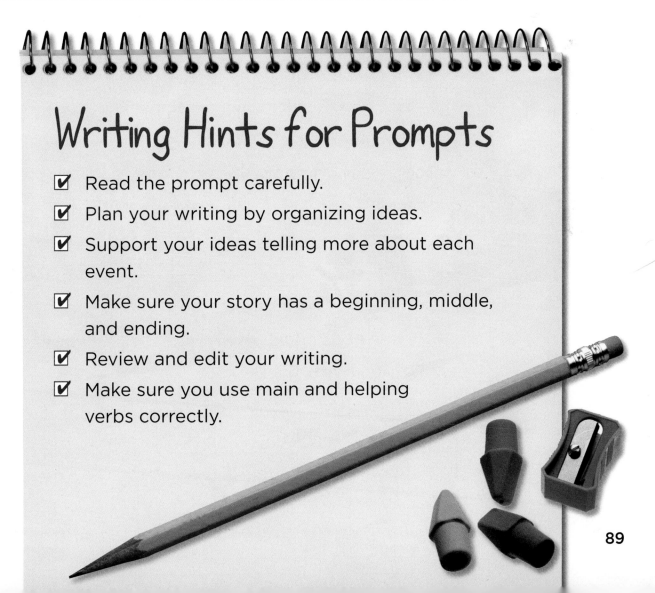

Writing Hints for Prompts

- ☑ Read the prompt carefully.
- ☑ Plan your writing by organizing ideas.
- ☑ Support your ideas telling more about each event.
- ☑ Make sure your story has a beginning, middle, and ending.
- ☑ Review and edit your writing.
- ☑ Make sure you use main and helping verbs correctly.

GETTING INVOLVED

Talk About It

What are some ways that you can help your school or community?

LOG ON Find out more about getting involved at **www.macmillanmh.com**

GORILLA GARDEN

by Michael Feldman

Have you ever taken a **tour** of a zoo? If so, it's likely that the person who led you through the zoo helped you to learn a lot about the animals.

Amelia Rinas is a high school student who lives in Ohio. One day Amelia visited the Cleveland Metroparks Zoo. She worried about the gorillas she saw there. She wondered if they were getting the right foods.

Amelia read all she could about gorillas and learned what they like to eat. Then she started a "gorilla garden." She grows the fruits and vegetables that gorillas love to eat. Some of those foods are tomatoes, carrots, and strawberries. Amelia works with other **volunteers** in her **community** who use their extra time to help Amelia and the gorillas. When they take the food to the zoo, the gorillas are **thrilled**. They look so excited!

Who is responsible for Amelia's interest in animals? Amelia is a member of Roots & Shoots. Its members are young people who care about animals and the environment. They helped Amelia understand that animals need our care, too. The **slogan** on the Roots & Shoots Web site is "Inspire, take action, make a difference." These words tell what the group is all about. The group urges kids and **grownups**, including parents and teachers, to do what they can to make a difference where they live.

Amelia believes that both people and animals **deserve** to be treated well.

When **interviewed** about her project, Amelia said, "I joined Roots & Shoots because I wanted to make a difference in the world."

There are many ways to make a difference in the world. Amelia Rinas's gorilla garden has helped make gorillas happier and healthier.

Reread for **Comprehension**

FCAT

Monitor Comprehension

Author's Purpose An author writes to entertain, inform, or explain. Usually, an author will give readers **clues** that help readers figure out the **author's purpose**. You can help monitor your understanding of an article by thinking about the author's purpose. Reread the article. Use your Author's Purpose Chart to figure out why the author wrote this article.

Clues

↓

Author's Purpose

Comprehension

Genre
Nonfiction Articles give information about real people, places, or things.

Monitor Comprehension

FCAT Author's Purpose

As you read, use your Author's Purpose Map.

Clues

↓

Author's Purpose

Read to Find Out
Why did the author write about Angel?

94

Here's My Dollar

By Gary Soto

Award Winning Author

Angel poses with her cat.

How tall is a hero? If you had ever met nine-year-old Angel Arellano, you'd know a hero is four feet two inches tall. Angel's story began on Thanksgiving Day. She was in the kitchen listening to her Great-Grandmother Sandy.

"The zoo has money problems," Great-Grandmother Sandy remarked.

Angel listened. She heard that Fresno's Chaffee Zoo didn't have enough money to take care of its animals. Angel wondered what would happen to the elephants, the hippo, and her favorite reptile, the boa constrictor.

Angel loved animals. She planned to study them and become a zoologist when she grew up. In their own apartment in Fresno, Angel's family had four cats—Buster, Krystal, Rex, and Oreo. Angel took good care of them and made sure that they always had food and water.

FCAT Author's Purpose
Why does the author tell us about Angel's pets?

Angel holds a skink at the Chaffee Zoo.

Angel felt sorry for the zoo animals. While the **grownups** were cooking Thanksgiving dinner, Angel was cooking up a way to help the animals. She decided to write a letter to show how she felt.

When she finished writing, Angel showed the letter to her mom and her aunt. They changed some of the words and fixed the spelling. Then Angel copied her letter onto fancy stationery and added a **slogan** at the bottom: "Give a dollar, save a life." She slipped a dollar into the envelope and addressed it to *The Fresno Bee*, the local newspaper.

Angel's letter to *The Fresno Bee*

Dear Fresno bee,

Thanksgiving day

My name is angel and I am nine. I heard that the Chaffee zoo is having money problems. I am very worried for the animals. I am worried because they might not have enough food or water of even might not have a home. They deserve to have a home and be safe and warm. I think that if everybody in Fresno gave $1.00 to the chaffee zoo it would help alot. Here's my dollar.

Angelica
Arellano
age 9
Fresno

Give a dollar save a life

97

Angel hoped that other people might send a dollar, too, after they had read her letter. She didn't know that the zoo needed three million dollars, but that wouldn't have stopped her anyhow. Angel was a girl on a mission!

A week later, a man from *The Fresno Bee* came to take a picture of Angel. A few days after that, Angel's letter was published in *The Fresno Bee*. Almost immediately, people began sending in checks and dollar bills. Angel's letter was working!

Child's Call to Aid the Zoo

Angel Arellano collects money for the Chaffee Zoo.

By Jim Davis

Nine-year-old Angel Arellano is sparking a grass-roots effort to help the Chaffee Zoo through its financial plight. The little girl sent a letter to *The Bee* and enclosed a $1 donation for the zoo. She asked others to donate as well. "I just hope it will help," Angel said. "I want the animals to be safe and warm and let them get fed like my letter said." Dozens have followed Angel's lead, sending donations ranging from $1 to a $1,000 check that arrived Thursday. After just two days' mail, the zoo has received $5,084.

Text from an article about Angel in *The Fresno Bee*, December 6, 2003

Hippos love the zoo's shallow river.

At school, Angel went to each classroom to read the letter that appeared in the newspaper. She asked her schoolmates to give money to the zoo. An empty water jug was placed in each classroom and in the main office. Students—and parents—began to fill the jugs with coins and dollar bills.

Angel's letter had touched the **community** of Fresno—and beyond. Donations for the Chaffee Zoo began to arrive from all over California. One donation came from as far away as England. It seemed as if the whole world wanted to help the zoo.

Angel feeds an apple to Angolia, the giraffe.

The people at the Chaffee Zoo were **thrilled**. They invited Angel and her family to the zoo. They wanted to thank Angel in person and give her a private **tour**.

At the zoo, Angel fed grapes to the chimpanzees. She fed the hippo and the buffalo, too. In a daring mood, Angel placed a slice of apple in her mouth. She stretched her neck toward Angolia, the giraffe, who leaned its long neck down and swiped the apple from her mouth!

Angel went on being a regular kid—for a while. Before long, she was asked to make public appearances to talk about the zoo. The zoo still needed money, and Angel was happy to help. The principal of her school drove her to other schools in the area. He was just as concerned about the zoo animals as Angel.

"The zoo needs your help," Angel told the other children. "We can all make a difference."

During these appearances, Angel autographed pieces of paper, posters, and lots of shirts and caps. When reporters **interviewed** her, she tried to be herself. She spoke from her heart.

Angel prepares to make a public service announcement.

Next, Angel was asked to appear on television. She was invited to be on a popular talk show. Angel flew from Fresno to Los Angeles. It was the first time she was ever on a plane!

At the television studio, Angel entered the stage to applause and her favorite rock music. She smiled and waved. The audience was rooting for her. They were rooting for the zoo animals back in Fresno, too.

More donations arrived after Angel's appearance on television. The Chaffee Zoo got larger and larger checks. One was for $10,000. Another was for $15,000. And one was for $50,000!

Of course, many donations were still just for one dollar. Children were sending in what they had, just as Angel had done on Thanksgiving Day.

Angel boards a plane to make a television appearance.

Zookeeper Mary helps Angel hold a boa constrictor.

Everyone was behind Angel and the zoo. High school teams held car washes to raise money. **Volunteers** showed up at the zoo to help paint and clean up. A local business made T-shirts with a picture of the zoo on the front.

The zookeepers were very happy. Ray Navarro is the person most responsible for the animals. He has hauled thousands of buckets of water for the animals. He has pushed wheelbarrows of hay for the elephants, the giraffes, and the zebras. "Angel opened the eyes of Fresno," said Ray. "She made us see that people can make a difference."

FCAT Author's Purpose
Why did the author choose to write about Angel?

103

Angel's fundraising efforts are
displayed on a billboard at the zoo.

The campaign started with a single dollar from Angel. In six months, the Chaffee Zoo received more than $600,000. The zoo has used some of the money to fix the pathway to the reptile house where the boa constrictor lives. It has also put in cushioned floors in the giraffe barn, plastered the seal pool, and fixed the rain forest bridge. Buildings have been painted and repaired, too.

The campaign to save the Chaffee Zoo has been exciting. People from Fresno are proud that a young girl woke up their own community spirit. The zoo is looking better and better. And even though the zoo animals can't speak human languages, if they could, they might say, "You are a hero to us, Angel Arellano. You **deserve** our thanks for saving our zoo."

The zoo's seals enjoy a swim in a newly plastered pool, thanks to Angel.

Here's Our Author

Gary Soto was born and raised in Fresno, California, which is also the hometown of the Chaffee Zoo. He has written many poems and stories for children and adults. In his spare time, Gary loves to read, play tennis and basketball, and travel. He still visits Fresno often, and there is a library named for him at Winchell Elementary School in Fresno.

Other books by Gary Soto: *Baseball in April* and *Chato's Kitchen*

LOG ON Find out more about Gary Soto at www.macmillanmh.com

FCAT **Author's Purpose**

Suppose you were the author of "Here's My Dollar." Describe why you wrote this article and how you achieved your goal. Use details from the article in your answer.

FCAT Comprehension Check

Summarize

Summarize "Here's My Dollar." Use your Author's Purpose Chart to help you.

Clues

↓

Author's Purpose

Think and Compare

1. Why do you think Gary Soto wrote "Here's My Dollar"? Use examples and information from the article in your answer. **Monitor Comprehension: Author's Purpose**

2. Reread pages 97–99. Explain how Angel "touched the community" of Fresno and beyond. How did *The Fresno Bee* help do this? Use article details in your answer. **Analyze**

3. Think of a good cause in your own community that needs help, such as a school, library, or park. How would you encourage people to help? **Apply**

4. Why is using a **slogan** a good way to help raise money for a cause? Use information from the story to support your ideas. **Synthesize**

5. Reread "Gorilla Garden" on pages 92–93. How are Amelia and Angel alike? Describe the different ways they help animals. **Reading/ Writing Across Texts**

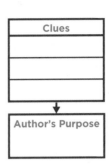

Neighbors

Poetry

Poetry uses rhyme, rhythm, and repetition to express feelings and ideas.

Literary Elements

A **Rhyme Scheme** is the pattern of rhymes in the last words of lines.

Repetition happens when words or phrases are repeated throughout a poem. A line that is repeated throughout is called a **refrain**.

The last line of each stanza is the refrain.

When I had the sniffles,

Your mom sent me stew.

You needed a project.

My daddy helped you.

Your dad helps us paint from ceiling to floor.

Neighbors are friends who live just next door.

I call you up

When I know you feel down.

When Fluffy was lost,

We looked all over town.

It's my turn to rake when your arms get
   too sore.

Neighbors are friends who live just next door.

—Mari Paz Pradillo

Recycling

Tucker Connors collected the papers

And Maya Ling tied them with string

Maya helped Tucker carry the papers

All the way to the recycling bins

Won Tan collected the cans

And Ruby Dean washed them all clean

Ruby helped Won carry the cans

All the way to the recycling bins

When we recycle, we help the plants

We help the creatures, from eagles to ants

We help make the world a healthier place

For one and for all in the human race

—J. Z. Belle

Plants and *ants* rhyme, as do *place* and *race*. The rhyme scheme for this stanza is AA BB.

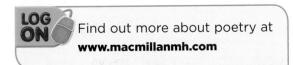

FCAT Connect and Compare

1. What are some repetitions in "Recycling"? **Repetition**

2. What does the poet want to tell you about neighbors? **Analyze**

3. Compare these two poems about helping and *Here's My Dollar*. How are these selections alike? How are they different? **Reading/Writing Across Texts**

LOG ON Find out more about poetry at www.macmillanmh.com

Writer's Craft

FCAT **A Strong Opening**

Good writers include a **strong opening** that grabs the reader's attention. A strong opening may be an interesting quote, question, or description.

I began with a question to grab my reader's attention.

I wrote directly to other kids who care about skateboarding.

No Place to Skateboard

by Carol L.

Do you dream of halfpipes and ramps? I do, but there is one problem. My town does not have a skateboard park. I think this is a big problem. Dad said I should write a letter to our mayor. I wrote and told him why I think a skateboard park would be a good and safe place where kids could have fun. Yesterday the mayor wrote back and said that he liked my idea. Now my town is going to build a special park for skateboarding. If I had not written that letter, nothing would have happened! Maybe you can write a letter and make your community better, too.

Writing Prompt

People often make their communities better by suggesting or planning changes.

Think about a problem in your community.

Now write about how you would solve this problem in your community.

FCAT Writer's Checklist

✓ **Focus:** I write clearly about my topic.

✓ **Organization:** First I tell about the problem. Then I explain how I would solve it.

☑ **Support:** I include a **strong opening** to grab the reader's attention.

✓ **Conventions:** I use homophones and irregular verbs correctly. All the words are spelled correctly.

Talk About It

If you could have a place of your own, where would it be and what would it look like?

LOG ON Find out more about creating special places at **www.macmillanmh.com**

A PLACE OF MY OWN

Pond Street Clubhouse

by Sylvia Medrano

On Saturday I went to the lumberyard with Dad to order lumber for the new garage. I saw the wood and got an idea.

"Hey, Dad," I said. "Could we build a clubhouse?"

"Probably not," said Dad. "I'll be too busy with the garage."

"But, Dad," I said, "you had a clubhouse when you were young."

Dad said, "I know, but first we have to build the garage."

I had to think of a way to get Dad to agree. "We can **separate** the clubhouse into two rooms," I said with **determination**. "One can be used as a **storage** room."

114

Dad thought about it for a moment. Then he said, "Let's wait to see if there is enough extra wood."

The garage supplies came the following weekend. There were huge piles of wood and a big box. It was a **crate** of nails and shingles for the roof. It looked like more than enough. When the truck left, Dad said, "Good news! We'll be able to build your clubhouse with the leftover wood when the garage is finished."

After a few weeks, it was time to start. A bunch of neighborhood kids came to help.

Dad let us measure the wood. Measuring has to be **exact** or else the pieces won't fit together. If Dad cut the wood too long or too short, our plans could be **ruined**. I knew we couldn't buy any extra wood.

When the clubhouse was finally finished, I was so thrilled. I made a sign and nailed it on the door. It said, "Pond Street Clubhouse—Welcome!" Now I have a great place to play. Am I the **luckiest** kid in town, or what?

Reread for **Comprehension**

Monitor Comprehension

FCAT **Plot Development** One way to monitor, or check, your understanding of plot in a story is to **make predictions**. You can make predictions about what characters might do or what events might happen. Reread the selection. Use your Predictions Chart to keep track of your predictions about characters and events. Then check to see if your predictions were correct by writing **what happens**.

What I Predict	What Happens

Comprehension

Genre

Realistic Fiction is an invented story that could have happened in real life.

Monitor Comprehension

FCAT **Plot Development**
As you read, use your Predictions Chart.

What I Predict	What Happens

Read to Find Out

How does the girl get her own room?

My Very Own Room

Award Winning Selection

by Amada Irma Pérez
illustrated by Maya Christina Gonzalez

I woke up one morning on a crowded bed in a crowded room. Víctor's elbow was jabbing me in the ribs. Mario had climbed out of his crib and crawled in with us. Now his leg lay across my face and I could hardly breathe. In the bed next to ours my three other brothers were sleeping.

I was getting too big for this. I was almost nine years old, and I was tired of sharing a room with my five little brothers. More than anything in the whole world I wanted a room of my own.

A little space was all I wanted, but there wasn't much of it. Our tiny house was shared by eight of us, and sometimes more when our friends and relatives came from Mexico and stayed with us until they found jobs and places to live.

Once a family with eight kids (mostly boys!) lived with us for two months. It was noisy and a lot of fun. There was always a long line to use the bathroom, but the toilet seat was always warm.

Sometimes very early in the morning while everyone was still sleeping, I would climb up the crooked ladder that leaned against the elm tree in our backyard. I would sit on a little board, pretending it was a bench, and just think. I could hear my father snoring. He worked all night at the factory and went to bed just before dawn.

I loved my brothers. It wasn't that I didn't want to be near them. I just needed a place of my own.

I tiptoed around our tiny, two bedroom house. I peeked behind the curtain my mother had made from flour sacks to **separate** our living room from the **storage** closet.

"Aha! This is it! This could be my room." I imagined it with my own bed, table, and lamp—a place where I could read the books I loved, write in my diary, and dream.

I sat down among the boxes. My mother must have heard me because she came in from the kitchen.

FCAT Plot Development

What will the girl try to do with the storage closet?

122

"Mamá, it's perfect," I said, and I told her my idea.
"Ay, *mijita*, you do not understand. We are storing
my sister's sewing machine and your uncle's garden
tools. Someday they will need their things to make
a better living in this new country. And there's the
furniture and old clothes," she said. Slowly she shook
her head.

Then she saw the **determination** on my face and the tears forming in my eyes. "Wait," she said, seriously thinking. "Maybe we could put these things on the back porch and cover them with old blankets."

"And we could put a tarp on top so nothing would get **ruined**," I added.

"Yes, I think we can do it. Let's take everything out and see how much space there is."

I gave her a great big hug and she kissed me.

After breakfast we started pushing the old furniture out to the back porch. Everyone helped. We were like a mighty team of powerful ants.

We carried furniture, tools, and machines. We dragged bulging bags of old clothes and toys. We pulled boxes of treasures and overflowing junk. Finally, everything was out except for a few cans of leftover paint from the one time we had painted the house.

Each can had just a tiny bit of paint inside. There was pink and blue and white, but not nearly enough of any one color to paint the room.

"I have an idea," I said to my brothers. "Let's mix them!" Héctor and Sergio helped me pour one can into another and we watched the colors swirl together. A new color began to appear, a little like purple and much stronger than pink. Magenta!

We painted and painted until we ran out of paint.

127

Mamá showed me how to measure my new magenta wall with a piece of bright yellow yarn left over from the last baby blanket she had crocheted. Tío Pancho was going back to Mexico and said I could have his bed, but we had to let him know if it would fit.

We cut off the piece of yarn that showed us just how big the bed could be. We all ran to Tío Pancho's waving the piece of yarn. We measured his bed. Perfect! That yellow piece of yarn was magical.

A little later Tío Pancho arrived with my new bed tied to the roof of his car. I ran out and hugged him. Papá helped him carry the bed in and carefully ease it into place.

My brothers jumped up and down and everybody clapped. Then Raúl moved an empty wooden crate over to my new bed and stood it on end to make a bedside table.

"All you need now is a little lamp," my mother said.

She brought out a shoe box stuffed with Blue Chip stamps she had been collecting for years. Mamá and Papá got them for free when they bought food or gas. They were like little prizes that could be used as money at special stores. But before we could spend them, we had to paste them into special stamp books.

We licked and licked and pasted and pasted. When we were done, Papá drove us to the stamp store.

FCAT **Plot Development**
What will the girl do with the Blue Chip stamps?

131

I saw the lamp I wanted right away. It was as dainty as a beautiful ballerina, made of white ceramic glass with a shade that had ruffles around the top and bottom.

I shut my eyes. I was so excited yet so afraid we wouldn't have enough stamps to get it. Then I heard my mother's voice. "Yes, *mijita*. We have enough."

When we got home, I carefully set the new lamp on my bedside table. Then I lay on my new bed and stared at the ceiling, thinking. Something was still missing, the most important thing …

Books!

The next day I went to our public library and rushed home with my arms full of books, six to be **exact**. It was my lucky number because there were six children in my family.

That evening, I turned on my new lamp and read and read. My two littlest brothers, Mario and Víctor, stood in the doorway holding back the flour-sack curtain. I invited them in. They cuddled up on my new bed and I read them a story. Then we said goodnight and they went back to their room.

I felt like the **luckiest**, happiest little girl in the whole world. Everyone in our family had helped to make my wish come true. Before I could even turn out the light, I fell asleep peacefully under a blanket of books in my very own room.

Amada and Maya's Room

Author Amada Irma Pérez grew up in a family just like the one in this story. Because her parents were unable to get the family a bigger house, there was not much room for Amada and her five brothers. But they did give Amada and her brothers lots of love and encouraged them to study and work hard.

Another book **by Amada Irma Pérez:**
My Diary from Here to There/Mi diario de aquí hasta allá

Illustrator Maya Christina Gonzalez has always loved to draw and paint. She has also always been very proud of being Mexican. In fact, as a child, Maya would draw her face on the blank page in the back of books because she wanted someone in the books to look like her.

 Find out more about Amada Irma Pérez and Maya Christina Gonzalez at **www.macmillanmh.com**

FCAT Author's Purpose

What was the author's purpose for writing *My Very Own Room*? Did Amada Irma Pérez want to entertain or inform? Use details from the story in your answer.

Summarize

Summarize *My Very Own Room*. Use your Predictions Chart to help you tell about events in the story that you predicted and what actually happens.

What I Predict	What Happens

Think and Compare

1. What story details help you predict whether the girl will get a room of her own? Use your Predictions Chart to help you answer. **Monitor Comprehension: Plot Development**

2. Reread pages 119–123 of *My Very Own Room*. What kind of relationship does the girl have with her family? How do you know? Use story details to support your answer. **Analyze**

3. What are some reasons why you might want a quiet space of your own? **Evaluate**

4. Why is it good for a whole family to help one family member with a problem? **Apply**

5. Reread "Pond Street Clubhouse" on pages 114–115. Think about how the main character is like the girl in *My Very Own Room*. Why is **determination** an important character trait in both characters? **Reading/Writing Across Texts**

Matter Matters!

by Karen O'Malley

Everything you see in your classroom is made of **matter**. Books, desks, pencils, and even you and the other students all take up space. Every object you see is an example of matter.

Properties of Matter

Not all matter is the same. You can describe matter and compare it with other types of matter by looking at its properties. A **property** is a characteristic that you can see or measure. Color and shape are properties. Look around your classroom at all the colors and shapes of the matter you see.

Measuring Matter

You can compare matter by measuring it. Look at your desk. Use a ruler to measure the sides. This will tell you the length and width.

You can also describe an object by looking at its **mass**. Mass tells how much matter is in an object. A heavy object has more mass than a light object. You can measure mass with a balance or scale.

Comparing Mass

A larger item does not always have more mass than a smaller one. Think about a beach ball and a bowling ball. Both objects take up about the same amount of space. However, the bowling ball has a much greater mass.

In the bowling ball, the tiny pieces of matter are packed more tightly than the matter in the beach ball. This is why the bowling ball is heavier. Now you know why a bowling ball is heavy enough to knock down the bowling pins. A beach ball could never do that!

These objects are about the same size. Which has the greater mass?

An Encyclopedia Article

Reading an Encyclopedia Article

Encyclopedia articles are arranged alphabetically in each volume, or book.

page number   guide word   heading   caption

103   Caliper

Caliper

A caliper is an instrument that measures the thickness or diameter of an object. It has a fixed arm and a second arm that moves along a graduated scale.

Uses of calipers

Calipers are used by orange

This caliper measures the diameter of the orange with a precise number. Farmers read the measurement on a digital display.

growers in Florida. Growers need to know whether the size of the fruit in of their crops stays the same, increases, or decreases. Calipers are useful because they can measure very small changes in the size of the oranges.

This article is from Volume C of an encyclopedia.

Measuring Mass and Volume

You can measure mass in different ways. For small, light objects, the unit of measurement is a gram (g). For larger, heavier objects, you use a kilogram (kg).

You measure liquids by volume. **Volume** is how much space the liquid takes up. Liquids are measured in measuring cups called beakers. The units of measure are milliliter (ml) and liter (L).

Measuring matter is an important part of the job for scientists, cooks, electricians, and many workers. For people who use measurement every day, the mass and volume of matter really matter!

Each of these paper clips has a mass of about 1 gram.

 FCAT Connect and Compare

1. Why are calipers a useful measurement tool for Florida orange growers? **Reading an Encyclopedia Article**

2. According to the article, what unit of measurement could you use to describe the weight of an elephant? A handful of sand? A jug of water? **Analyze**

3. In *My Very Own Room*, how did the family know the bed would fit in the storage space? **Reading Across Texts**

Science Activity

List different ways you can measure the length of an object if you do not have a ruler. Hint: Think about how the main character and her mother measure the bed in *My Very Own Room*.

 Find out more about measurement at **www.macmillanmh.com**

143

Write Directions

Writer's Craft

FCAT Time-Order Words

Words such as *first*, *next*, *then*, and *last* tell the order in which things happen. Writers use these **time-order words** to show the sequence in which things should be done.

I used time-order words to show the sequence in which things should be done.

I completed my directions with the time-order word "last."

How to Make a Study Place

by Robert H.

Studying for a test is easier when you have a quiet place of your own. Here's how to make one. First, find a chair that's comfortable and put it in a quiet corner that isn't too close to the TV, radio, or phone. Next, get a healthful snack so you'll think about studying, not sandwiches. Then, gather the materials you'll need. The last thing to do is to tell everyone in the house that you need peace and quiet.

Writing Prompt

People often write directions in order to explain how to do or make something.

Think about something you know how to do or make.

Now write directions explaining how to do or make something.

FCAT Writer's Checklist

 Focus: I write clearly about one topic.

 Organization: I include **time-order words**, such as *first* and *last*, that show the sequence of the steps in my directions.

 Support: I use specific words and details in my steps.

 Conventions: I use contractions correctly. All my words are spelled correctly.

FCAT

Review

Draw Conclusions

Compare and Contrast

Author's Purpose

Context Clues

Multiple-Meaning
 Words

Time Line

World Cup Worries

Fabio was all set to watch the World Cup match. His favorite team was playing—Brazil. Just as he sat down, Fabio's father called, "Fabio, come here, please."

"But Dad, the World Cup is starting!" cried Fabio.

"That may be," said Mr. Silva. "But that doesn't change the fact that you have chores to do."

Work during the big match? Fabio really wanted to ignore his father and watch the game. He decided that if he did his chores really fast, he could still catch most of the match.

"What do you need me to do, Dad?" asked Fabio.

"You can start by cleaning your room," Mr. Silva said.

"Okay," said Fabio. He was relieved because he knew he could get that job done fast. He threw clothes in the hamper, put books on the bookshelf, and straightened up his shoes. In 20 minutes, his room looked tidy—sort of.

"I'm done, Dad!" yelled Fabio. He hurried into the other room to turn on the television.

"Great," said Mr. Silva. "Now you can help me with the yard work."

Fabio sighed. He knew that yard work could take the rest of the day. "Dad, that means we'll miss the whole match!"

"This is more important," said Mr. Silva. He gave Fabio some gardening gloves and some trash bags, and put him to work cleaning up.

"Dad, I thought you loved watching the World Cup," said Fabio.

"I do," said Mr. Silva, "but work should be done while the sun shines."

After a few hours of hard work, Mr. Silva said that it was time for a break. Fabio was gloomy since he'd missed the whole match. He barely said a word as his father fixed him a snack.

"Fabio, I know you wanted to watch the match," said Mr. Silva. "I appreciate that you made the choice to help me, instead."

"I'm not sure I had a choice, Dad," replied Fabio.

"You can always choose to do the wrong thing," explained his father, "but you didn't. Now, here's the good news. I taped the game while we worked. Let's watch it while we eat!"

"All right! That sounds like a great choice, Dad," laughed Fabio.

Susan B. Anthony

A Pioneer for Women's Rights

SUSAN B. ANTHONY was born to a Quaker family. Quakers believe in justice and fair treatment for everyone. In the early 1800s, most girls were not given an education equal to that of boys, but the Quakers allowed both boys and girls to have equal educations. In religious meetings both Quaker girls and boys could speak out. And women could vote on church matters.

After Susan B. Anthony met Elizabeth Cady Stanton, they became close friends and leaders in the women's suffrage movement. The suffrage movement worked to get women the right to vote. Anthony and Stanton were a great team. Their goal was to change the United States Constitution and give women the right to vote.

In 1872, Anthony brought 15 women to vote in a

Women Can Vote!

This time line shows important dates in Susan B. Anthony's life and in the women's suffrage movement.

Susan B. Anthony born February 15		Arrested for voting		Meets President Theodore Roosevelt
1820	**1851**	**1872**	**1881**	**1905**
	Meets Elizabeth Cady Stanton		Writes book about women's rights	

national election. She was arrested. At her trial the judge said that Anthony did not have the right to vote. Anthony refused to pay the $100 fine.

Anthony continued to work for women's suffrage throughout her life. She made many trips across the country and gave lectures about why women's rights were important. During her life Anthony published several newspapers. With Elizabeth Stanton and Matilda Gage, she wrote a book about the suffrage movement.

Susan B. Anthony died in 1906. In 1920 the Nineteenth Amendment was finally passed. This amendment gave women the right to vote. Because of all of Anthony's hard work, this law is sometimes called the Susan B. Anthony Amendment.

1906	1920	1920	1978
	19th Amendment passes		Susan B. Anthony dollar coin created
Dies March 13		Over eight million women vote	

MAKING MONEY

Let's Trade!

by Alex Ely

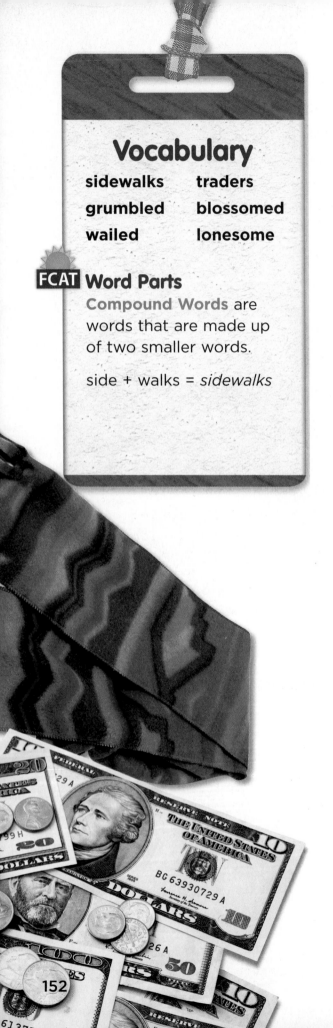

Vocabulary

sidewalks	traders
grumbled	blossomed
wailed	lonesome

FCAT **Word Parts**

Compound Words are words that are made up of two smaller words.

side + walks = *sidewalks*

Elizabeth and Danny walked along newly paved **sidewalks** on a frosty winter morning. Elizabeth wore a hat and gloves but no scarf. Danny wore a hat and two scarves, but he didn't have any gloves. Both of them were freezing.

"I'm so cold," Elizabeth **grumbled** under her breath.

"Me too," Danny **wailed**.

Then Elizabeth had an idea! "What if I traded you one glove for one of your scarves?" Elizabeth said. "Then both of our necks would be warm, and we'd each have one warm hand. We could put the other hand in our pockets."

"Good idea!" said Danny.

After they shared the scarf and glove, they began to feel warmer.

A few minutes later Mrs. Baxter appeared. "Did I just see you barter?" she asked.

Elizabeth and Danny looked puzzled. "What's barter?" Elizabeth asked.

613777

"Barter means trade," Mrs. Baxter explained. "You two traded a scarf and a glove so you could be warm. Did you know that **traders** bartered for thousands of years?"

"Really? How did it work?" Danny asked.

Mrs. Baxter said, "Well, traders who had too much of one thing, such as salt or cloth or pigs, would exchange them with other traders for other things that they needed. Trading grew and **blossomed**, but it had problems."

"Like what?" Elizabeth asked.

"Suppose you raised chickens. You could trade the chickens and eggs for what you needed. But if the chickens got away—"

"I wouldn't have anything to trade!"

"Exactly!" said Mrs. Baxter.

"And you'd be so **lonesome** without your poultry friends!" Danny said with a grin.

"Now you see why people began to use money to trade," Mrs. Baxter said.

"Is it true that silver and gold coins were used before paper money?" Danny asked.

"Yes, but they were too heavy to carry." Mrs. Baxter said. "People then began to write promises on paper instead of trading coins. That was how paper money got its start."

"Wow!" said Elizabeth. "But I guess people still trade sometimes, the way Danny and I did today!"

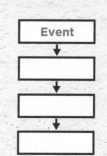

Reread for **Comprehension**

Summarize

FCAT **Chronological Order** Many stories are written in sequence, or **chronological order**. Knowing the sequence of **events** will help you better understand a story. You can summarize a story by paying close attention to the order in which the events happen. Reread the selection. Use your Sequence Chart to record the story's events in chronological order.

Event

Comprehension

Genre
Historical Fiction is a story in which fictional characters take part in actual historical events.

Summarize
Chronological Order

As you read, use your Sequence Chart.

Event
↓
↓
↓

Read to Find Out
How does Amanda help her town become a boom town?

154

BOOM TOWN

by Sonia Levitin

illustrated by Cat Bowman Smith

Award Winning Author

155

It took us twenty-one days on the stagecoach to get to California. When we got there, I thought we'd live with Pa in the gold fields. A whole tent city was built up. But Ma shook her head. "The gold fields are no place for children. We'll get a cabin and live in town."

What town? A stage stop, a pump house, a few log cabins— that was all. It was so wide and **lonesome** out west, even my shadow ran off.

Ma found a cabin big enough for all of us: Baby
Betsy, brothers Billy, Joe, Ted, and me—Amanda.
Pa came in from the gold fields every Saturday night,
singing:

"So I got me a mule
And some mining tools,
A shovel and a pick and a pan;

But I work all day
Without no pay.
I guess I'm a foolish man."

First Ma made him take a bath in a tin tub set out
under the stars. Then Pa sang songs and told stories
he'd heard from the miners—stories about men
finding big nuggets and striking it rich. But poor Pa,
he had no luck at all. Still, every Monday morning
he'd leave for the gold fields full of hope.

Days were long and lonely. The hills spread out as far as forever. Nights, me and Ma and my brothers and Baby Betsy would sit out and wait for a shooting star to sail across the sky. Once in a while a crow flew by. That's all the excitement there was.

My brothers worked up some furrows. They planted corn and potatoes and beans. Then they ran around climbing trees, skinning their knees. But after all the water was fetched and the wash was done, after the soap was made and the fire laid, after the beds were fixed and the floor was swept clean, I'd sit outside our cabin door with Baby Betsy, so bored I thought I'd die. Also, I hankered for some pie. I loved to bake pie.

I asked Ma and she said, "Pie would be good, but we have no pie pans and no real oven, just the wood stove. How would you bake a pie?"

I poked around in a big box of stuff and found an old iron skillet. I decided to make a pie crust and pick gooseberries to fill it.

Gooseberries grew on the bushes near town. I picked a big pailful and went back home. I made a crust with flour, butter, a little water, and a pinch of salt, and then I rolled it out.

Ma came in and said, "Looks good, Amanda. I knew you could make it. But tell me, how will you bake it?"

I showed Ma the skillet. She shook her head. "I don't think it will work, but you can try."

"It will work," I said.

FCAT Chronological Order

What steps does Amanda take to start baking her pie?

Brothers Billy and Joe and Ted stood there laughing. When the wood turned to coals, I pushed my pie inside the old stove. After a while I smelled a bad burning. I pulled out my pie, hard as a rock. Billy, Joe, and Ted whooped and slapped their sides. They snatched up my pie and tossed it high into the air. They ran outside and Billy whacked it hard with a stick. Pie pieces flew all over the place, and my brothers bent over, laughing.

I was so mad I went right back in to make another, and I swore none of them would get a bite. I rolled out my crust and filled it with berries, shoved the pie into the oven, and soon took it out.

I set the pie down to cool. I went off to do some mending. Next thing I knew, Baby Betsy, just learning to walk, sat there with pie goo all over her face. Too soft, the filling ran down on Betsy, and she **wailed** like a coyote in the night.

It took one more try, but I got it right. That night we ate my gooseberry pie, and it was delicious.

When Pa came home from the gold fields on Saturday night, there was a pie for him, too. "Amanda, you are the queen of the kitchen!" Pa scooped me up and whirled me around. I was proud.

The next week I made an extra pie for Pa to take with him to the gold fields.

Saturday night when he came home singing, coins jangled in his pocket.

We all ran out to ask, "Did you strike gold, Pa?"

"No," he said. "I sold Amanda's pie. The miners loved it. They paid me twenty-five cents a slice!"

After that, Pa took pies to the gold fields every week. And every week he came home with coins in his pockets. Some miners walked right to our door looking for pie. They told Ma, "You should open a bakery."

Ma said, "It's my girl Amanda who is the baker. If she wants to make pies, that's fine. But I have no time."

Ma had a new baby on the way. It was up to me. I figured I could sell pies to the miners and fill up our money jar.

But I needed help. I rounded up my brothers and told them, "If you want to eat pie, you've got to work."

They **grumbled** and groaned, but they knew I meant it. So Billy built me a shelf, Joe made a sign, AMANDA'S FINE PIES, and Ted helped pick berries and sour apples.

I needed more pans and another bucket. One day Peddler Pete came by, and with the money I'd made I bought them.

"You're a right smart little girl," said the peddler, "being in business like this."

I thought fast and told him, "Anybody can make money out here. Folks need things all the time, and there're no stores around. If you were to settle and start one, I'll bet you'd get rich."

Peddler Pete scratched his beard. "Not a bad idea," he said. "My feet are sore from roaming. I could use this cart and build my way up to having a store."

So pretty soon we had us a real store called PEDDLER PETE'S TRADING POST. Trappers and **traders** and travelers appeared. After shopping at Pete's, they were good and hungry.

They came to our cabin, looking for pie. Some liked it here so well they decided to stay. Soon we had a cooper, a tanner, a miller, a blacksmith. A town was starting to grow.

A prospector came in on the stage from St. Joe, his clothes covered with dirt. He looked around at the folks eating pie, and he asked, "Is there someone here who does washing?"

I stepped right up and I told him, "What we need is a laundry. Why don't you stay and start one? Why, the miners are sending their shirts clear to China. You'll make more money doing laundry than looking for gold."

The man thought a while, then said with a smile, "You're right, little lady. It's a dandy idea. I'll send for my wife to help."

Soon shirts and sheets fluttered on the line as people brought their washing in. A tailor came to make and mend clothes. A cobbler crafted shoes and boots. We heard the *tap tap* of his hammer and smelled the sweet leather. A barber moved in with shaving mugs, and an apothecary with herbs and healing drugs. So the town grew up all around us.

My pie business **blossomed**. Sometimes the line snaked clear around the house. Baby Betsy entertained the people while they waited. Billy added another shelf. Joe and Ted made a bench. We all picked berries and apples. Even Ma came to help. We had to get a bigger jar for all the money coming in.

One day our old friend Cowboy Charlie rode by. Like everyone else, he stopped for some pie. "I'd like to rest a spell," he said. "Where can I leave my horse for the night?"

"There's no livery stable," I said. "But why don't you start one? You'd rent out horses, and wagons too. That would be the perfect business for you."

"You're just full of great ideas, little lady," Cowboy Charlie said. He twirled his lariat. "I'd like to settle down. I'll stay here and do just that."

Soon a trail was worn right to Charlie's stable door. All day we heard the snorting of horses. Now Charlie needed hay. Farmers brought wagons and sacks full of feed. With all those people riding in, someone decided to build a hotel and a cafe. The town grew fast all around us.

The owner of the cafe bought pies from me, five or six at a time. I taught Billy how to roll the crust. Joe got wood for the stove. Ted washed the fruit, and Baby Betsy tried to stir in the sugar.

The money jar in our kitchen looked ready to bust. Where could we safely keep all that cash? Lucky us, one day Mr. Hooper, the banker, appeared.

"I'm building a bank," Mr. Hooper said to me. "This is getting to be a boom town."

"We'll use your bank," I told Mr. Hooper, "but the roads are so poor. In winter there's mud, and in summer there's dust. We need some **sidewalks** and better streets."

"You're a smart little lady," said Mr. Hooper, tipping his hat. "I'll see what I can do about that."

Before we knew it, the bank was built and wooden sidewalks were laid. One street was called Bank Street; the other was Main. Soon every lane and landmark had a name. Pa and my brothers built on a big room for our bakery.

Men sent for their families. New houses appeared everywhere. Babies and children filled up the town. We needed a school, and a good schoolmarm.

We knew Miss Camilla from our stagecoach days. She was living up the coast a ways. Cowboy Charlie rode off to fetch her, and she was glad to come.

Miss Camilla, the teacher, had married a preacher, and he came too. We all got together to build a church and a school. Bells rang out every day of the week. Now this was a real boom town!

One day Pa said to me, "Amanda, I'm through panning for gold. Will you let me be in business with you?"

"Sure!" I said, happily. "I'd love to work with you, Pa, and I'd also like to go to school."

FCAT Chronological Order

What is the order of events in the making of Amanda's boom town?

So Pa turned to baking, and we all worked together.
Pa sang while he rolled out the dough:

"Amanda found a skillet
And berries to fill it,
Made pies without a pan;

Our pies are the best
In all the West.
I guess I'm a lucky man."

Now Pa is with us every day. There's excitement
and bustle all around. Our house sits in the middle of
a boom town!

And to think it all started with me, Amanda, baking pies!

BANK ON SONIA AND CAT

AUTHOR
Sonia Levitin wrote this story after reading about a woman who made more than $10,000 by baking pies in a skillet during the California Gold Rush. Sonia loves research, so it is not surprising that she found such an interesting fact. History is just one of the things that Sonia likes to write about. She also writes mysteries, adventures, and funny stories.

ILLUSTRATOR
Cat Bowman Smith started out drawing magazine pictures. Her illustrations became very popular. Soon she was illustrating books. Today she has illustrated more than 40 of them.

LOG ON Find out more about Sonia Levitin and Cat Bowman Smith at **www.macmillanmh.com**

Other books by Sonia Levitin: *Nine for California* and *Taking Charge*

FCAT Author's Purpose

Did Sonia Levitin write to entertain or to explain how to do something? What clues help you figure out her purpose?

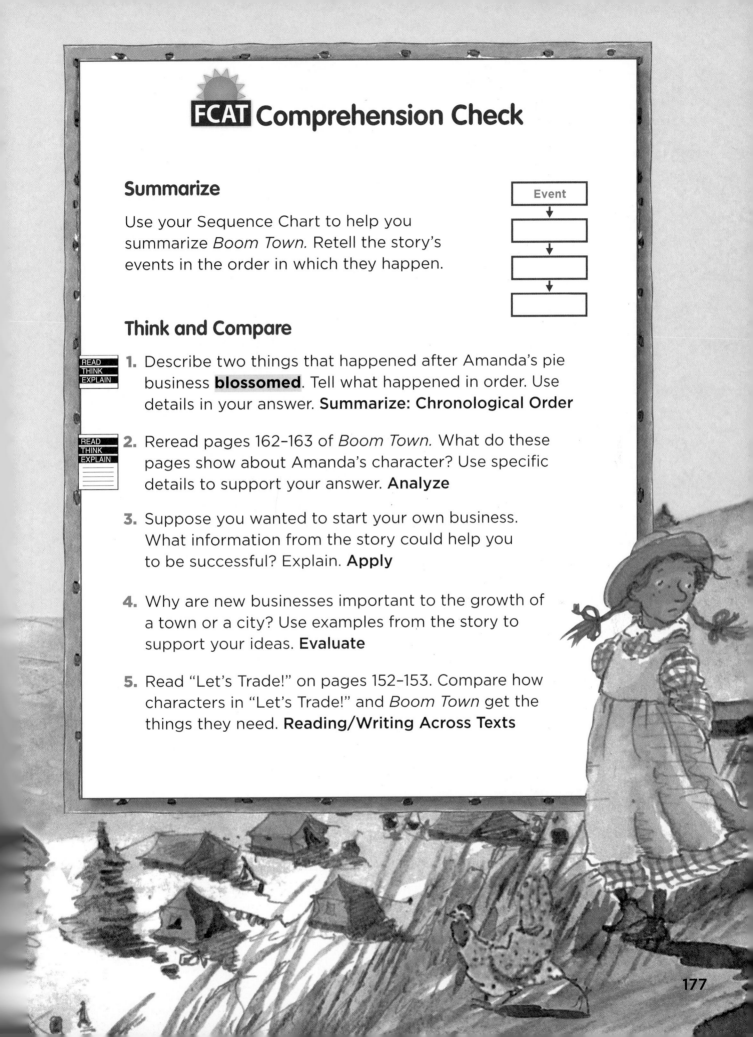

FCAT Comprehension Check

Summarize

Use your Sequence Chart to help you summarize *Boom Town.* Retell the story's events in the order in which they happen.

Event
↓
↓
↓

Think and Compare

READ THINK EXPLAIN

1. Describe two things that happened after Amanda's pie business **blossomed**. Tell what happened in order. Use details in your answer. **Summarize: Chronological Order**

READ THINK EXPLAIN

2. Reread pages 162–163 of *Boom Town.* What do these pages show about Amanda's character? Use specific details to support your answer. **Analyze**

3. Suppose you wanted to start your own business. What information from the story could help you to be successful? Explain. **Apply**

4. Why are new businesses important to the growth of a town or a city? Use examples from the story to support your ideas. **Evaluate**

5. Read "Let's Trade!" on pages 152–153. Compare how characters in "Let's Trade!" and *Boom Town* get the things they need. **Reading/Writing Across Texts**

How to Earn Money!

by R. J. Harkin

Would you like to do something new and exciting? Would you like to be looked up to and respected by kids and adults alike? Would you like to earn money in your free time? If you answered "Yes!" to any of these questions, then starting your own **business** might be right for you!

You Can Do It!

"My own business?" you might ask. "But I'm only a third-grader!" No problem! Even third-graders have plenty of talent and **services** to offer.

Do you enjoy cooking or baking? Then you may consider whipping up and selling a few **batches** of your fabulous blueberry muffins. Do you like arts and crafts? If so, you can make and sell artwork or jewelry. Do animals like you? Many busy families need responsible people to walk their dogs and feed their cats. The possibilities are endless! So, wash a car, plant a garden, or rake a lawn. If people want and need your special talents and services, you'll soon be in business!

Starting a Dog-Washing Business

Using a Calendar

A calendar is a kind of chart that organizes information in chronological order. A calendar can help you keep track of what you need to do.

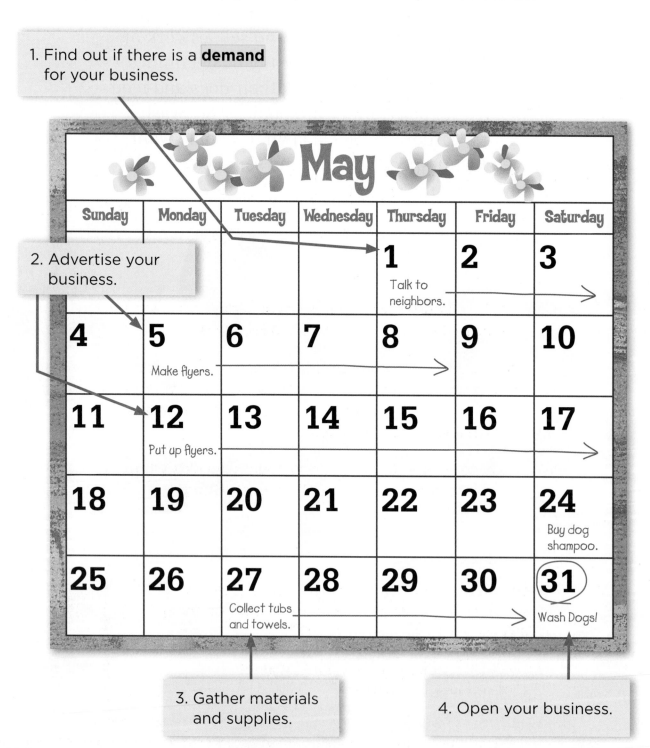

1. Find out if there is a **demand** for your business.

2. Advertise your business.

May

Sunday	Monday	Tuesday	Wednesday	Thursday	Friday	Saturday
				1 Talk to neighbors.	2	3 →
4	5 Make flyers.	6	7	8 →	9	10
11	12 Put up flyers.	13	14	15	16	17 →
18	19	20	21	22	23	24 Buy dog shampoo.
25	26	27 Collect tubs and towels.	28	29	30 →	(31) Wash Dogs!

3. Gather materials and supplies.

4. Open your business.

Connect and Compare

1. Look at the calendar on page 180. Which days are used for advertising? How will this be done? **Using a Calendar**

2. Suppose you live in a neighborhood where most people work all day. Many people are not home to cook, work in the yard, or spend time with their pets. What businesses might people want to use? **Apply**

3. What advice do you think Amanda could give kids who want to start a business today? **Reading/Writing Across Texts**

 Social Studies Activity

Research a business that interests you. Create a calendar that shows your preparations for opening that business.

 Find out more about businesses at
www.macmillanmh.com

Writer's Craft

FCAT Multiple Paragraphs

Multiple paragraphs should be written in a logical order. Each paragraph should begin with a topic sentence that states the main idea. The other sentences give supporting details.

Each paragraph begins with a topic sentence.

The details in each paragraph tell about the topic sentence.

How Much Alike Are We?

by Sarah A.

Amanda and I are different because she lived a long time ago and I live in modern times. Amanda and her family ride in stagecoaches. Today we travel in cars, trains, and airplanes. She wears dresses. I wear jeans.

Amanda and I are also the same. We are both girls who like to bake. Plus, Amanda starts a business, and I walk my neighbor's dogs. We both like people.

Amanda and I are probably more alike than we are different. We are both interested in many different things, and we both like to solve problems.

182

Writing Prompt

People may be both alike and different.

Think of two people you know who are alike and different.

Now explain how the two people you know are alike and different.

FCAT Writer's Checklist

 Focus: I clearly tell how things are alike and different.

 Organization: I use **multiple paragraphs**. Each paragraph begins with a topic sentence.

 Support: I choose details that tell about the topic sentences.

 Conventions: I use pronouns correctly. My words are spelled correctly.

Making a DIFFERENCE

Talk About It

Why is it important to help others?

LOG ON Find out more about helping others and making a difference at **www.macmillanmh.com**

An Armenian family with a cow

Helping People Help Themselves

by Zoe Tomasi

In the 1930s, Dan West was farming in Spain. It was wartime, and people were starving. As he handed out cups of milk to children, an idea hit him. "These children don't need a cup. They need a cow." This was the start of Heifer International.

Send Some Cows

Do you think a nice **gift** is a bike or CD? Heifer International gives different kinds of presents. Its presents might say "quack" or "moo." Dan West asked friends in the United States to give gifts of heifers, or young cows. Since then, Heifer International has given animals to four million families. It gives people the chance to feed themselves.

Pass on the Gift

Heifer International wants the people they help to help others. For one project, the group sent chickens to some children in Asia. The children **yearned** for the day when they could help others.

Nine-year-old Julie said, "I want other girls like me to take care of chickens and their families. I want to share and give many away."

Julie knew she had to **tend** to her chickens well so they would **produce** new eggs and healthy chicks. She took good care of them, and they gave birth to strong, **sturdy** chicks. Julie then passed on the gift of chicks to other families.

Letting Children Learn

Because of Heifer International, children can spend their days in a **schoolhouse** instead of working in the fields. They can use the money they earn from their animals to pay for school.

Heifer International has made a huge difference in people's lives for many years, thanks to a **kindhearted** farmer named Dan West.

This girl will care for her chicks so they grow up to be healthy.

Reread for Comprehension

Make Inferences and Analyze

Cause and Effect A **cause** is why something happens. The **effect** is what happens. Sometimes you need to analyze what happens in a story and make inferences about why these events happen. Reread the article. Use your Cause and Effect Chart to record causes and their effects.

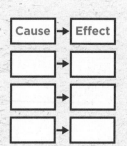

Cause	→	Effect
	→	
	→	
	→	

Comprehension

Genre

Narrative Nonfiction is a story that gives facts about actual people or situations.

Make Inferences and Analyze

FCAT Cause and Effect

As you read, use your Cause and Effect Chart.

Cause	→	Effect
	→	
	→	
	→	

Read to Find Out

How will Beatrice find a way to go to school?

Beatrice's Goat

by Page McBrier
illustrated by Lori Lohstoeter

Award Winning Author

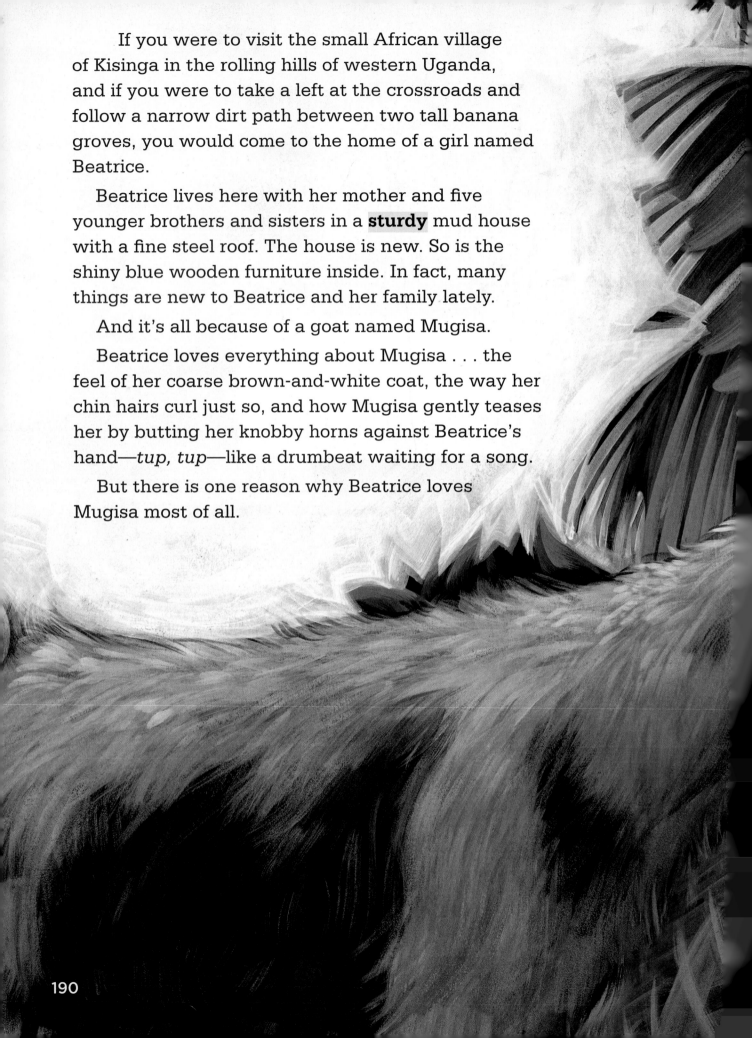

If you were to visit the small African village of Kisinga in the rolling hills of western Uganda, and if you were to take a left at the crossroads and follow a narrow dirt path between two tall banana groves, you would come to the home of a girl named Beatrice.

Beatrice lives here with her mother and five younger brothers and sisters in a **sturdy** mud house with a fine steel roof. The house is new. So is the shiny blue wooden furniture inside. In fact, many things are new to Beatrice and her family lately.

And it's all because of a goat named Mugisa.

Beatrice loves everything about Mugisa . . . the feel of her coarse brown-and-white coat, the way her chin hairs curl just so, and how Mugisa gently teases her by butting her knobby horns against Beatrice's hand—*tup, tup*—like a drumbeat waiting for a song.

But there is one reason why Beatrice loves Mugisa most of all.

In the time before Mugisa, Beatrice spent her days helping her mama hoe and plant in the fields, **tend** the chickens, watch the younger children, and grind the cassava flour that they would take to market to sell.

Once in a while, when she was tending baby Paskavia, Beatrice would stop by the **schoolhouse**. Often, the students had carried their long wooden benches outside to work under the cool shade of the jackfruit trees. Then Beatrice would stand quietly off to one side, pretending she was a student, too.

Oh, how she longed to be a schoolgirl! How she **yearned** to sit on one of the benches and figure sums on a small slate chalkboard. How she wished to turn the pages of a worn copybook and study each word over and over until it stuck in her mind like a burr.

"I'll never be able to go to school," she would sigh. "How could I ever save enough money to pay for books or a uniform?"

One day while Beatrice was busy pulling weeds, Mama came to her with dancing eyes. "Beatrice, some **kindhearted** people from far away have given us a lucky **gift**. We are one of twelve village families to receive a goat."

Beatrice was puzzled. A goat? What kind of gift was a goat? It couldn't get up each morning and start their charcoal fire for cooking. It couldn't hike down to the stream each week and scrub their dirty clothes clean. It couldn't keep an eye on Grace, Moses, Harriet, Joash, and Paskavia.

Her long fingers tugged patiently at the weeds. "That's very nice, Mama," she said politely.

Then Mama added, "It will be your job to take care of our goat. If you do, it can bring wonderful things."

Beatrice looked up at her mother. "Will this goat come soon?" she asked. "Because I would like to meet such a goat."

Mama laughed. "Good things take time. First I must plant pastures and build our goat a shed."

Beatrice nodded slowly. Surely Mama knew what she was doing. "I will help you," she declared.

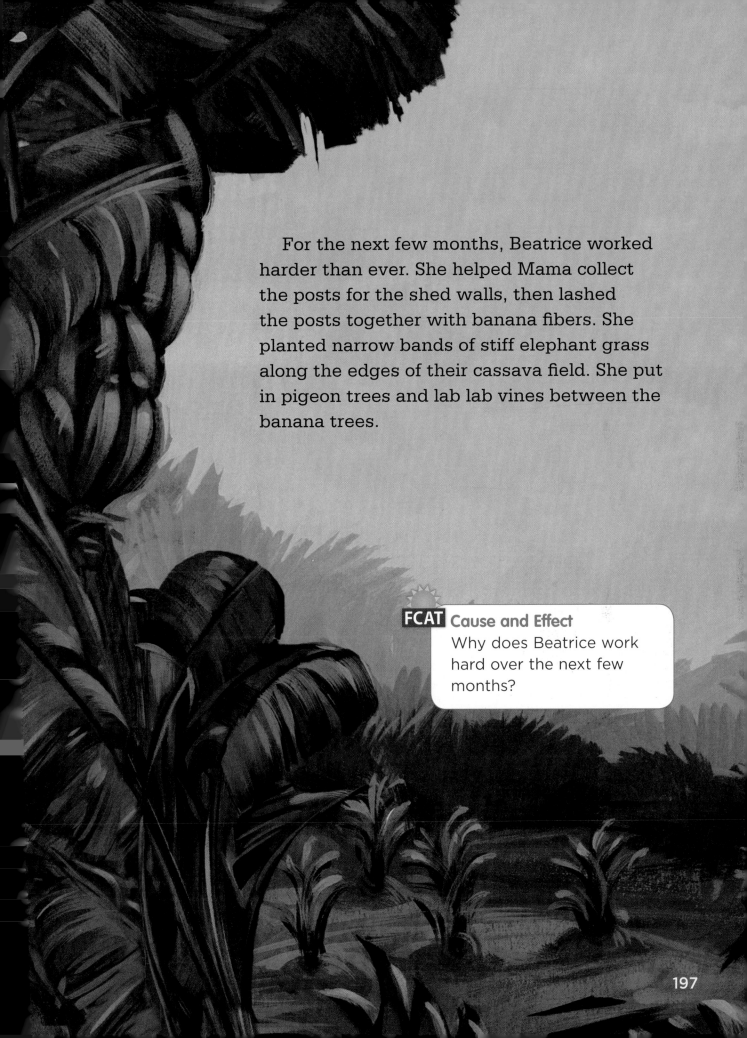

For the next few months, Beatrice worked harder than ever. She helped Mama collect the posts for the shed walls, then lashed the posts together with banana fibers. She planted narrow bands of stiff elephant grass along the edges of their cassava field. She put in pigeon trees and lab lab vines between the banana trees.

FCAT **Cause and Effect**
Why does Beatrice work hard over the next few months?

Finally, one day Beatrice's goat arrived, fat and sleek as a ripe mango. Beatrice stood shyly with her brothers and sisters, then stepped forward and circled the goat once. She knelt close, inspecting its round belly, and ran her hand along its smooth back. "Mama says you are our lucky gift," she whispered. "So that is what I will name you. *Mugisa* ... luck."

Two weeks later, Mugisa gave birth. It was Beatrice who discovered first one kid and then, to her surprise, another. "Twins!" she exclaimed, stooping down to examine them. "See that, my Mugisa? You have already brought us *two* wonderful things." Beatrice named the first kid *Mulindwa*, which means expected, and the second *Kihembo*, or surprise.

Each day Beatrice made sure Mugisa got extra elephant grass and water to help her **produce** lots of milk, even though it meant another long trip down to the stream and back.

When the kids no longer needed it, Beatrice took her own first taste of Mugisa's milk. "Mmm. Sweet," she said, mixing the rest into her cup of breakfast porridge. Beatrice knew Mugisa's milk would keep them all much healthier.

Now, each morning after breakfast, Beatrice would head off to the shed to sell whatever milk was left over. "Open for business," she would say, in case anyone was listening.

Often she would spy her friend Bunane coming through the banana groves.

"Good morning, Beatrice, Mugisa, Expected, and Surprise," Bunane would always say. Then he would hand Beatrice a tall pail that she would fill to the top with Mugisa's milk.

When Beatrice finished pouring, Bunane would hand her a shiny coin, and Beatrice would carefully tuck the money into the small woven purse at her side.

Day after day, week after week, Beatrice watched the purse get fuller. Soon there would be enough money for a new shirt for Moses and a warm blanket for the bed she shared with Grace.

FCAT Cause and Effect

How does Mugisa help Beatrice and her family?

One day, Beatrice returned from collecting water and noticed Mama frowning and counting the money in her woven purse. Beatrice put down the water can and rushed to her mother's side. "Mama! What is it?" she asked. "What's wrong?"

As she looked up, Mama's frown turned to a small smile. "I think," she said, "you may just have saved enough to pay for school."

"School?" Beatrice gasped in disbelief. "But what about all the other things we need?"

"First things first," Mama said.

Beatrice threw her arms around her mother's neck. "Oh, Mama, thank you." Then she ran to where her goat stood chewing her cud and hugged her tight. "Oh, Mugisa!" she whispered. "Today *I* am the lucky one. You have given me the gift I wanted most."

The very next week Beatrice started school. On the first morning that she was to attend, she sat proudly waiting for milk customers in her new yellow blouse and blue jumper, Mugisa by her side.

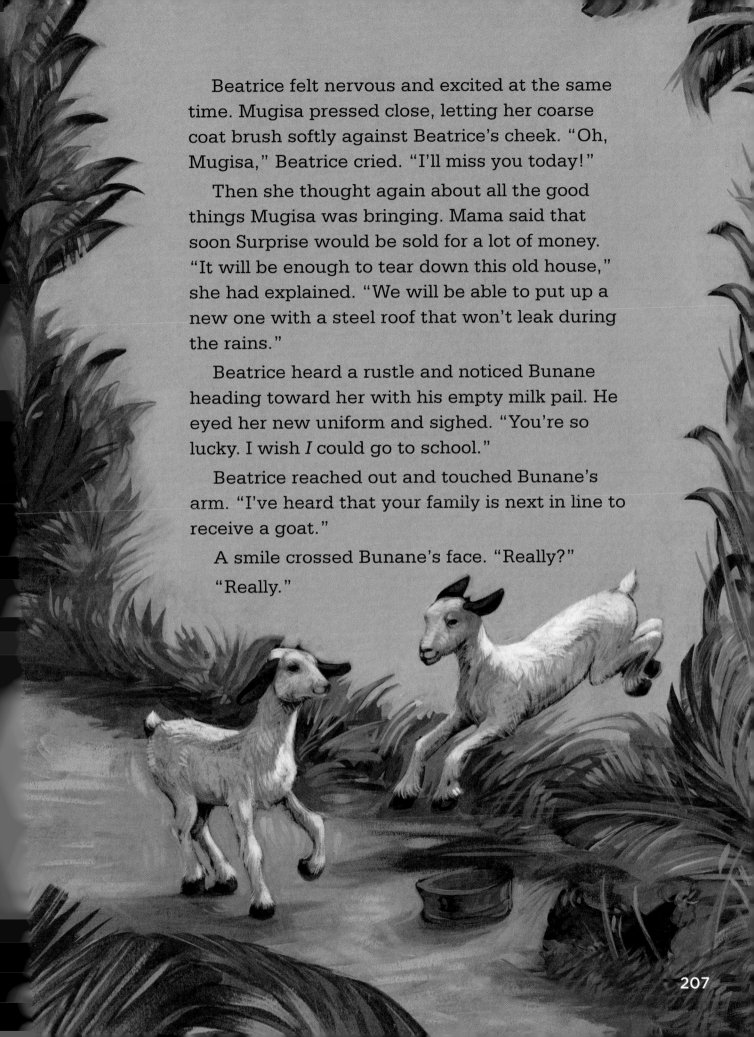

Beatrice felt nervous and excited at the same time. Mugisa pressed close, letting her coarse coat brush softly against Beatrice's cheek. "Oh, Mugisa," Beatrice cried. "I'll miss you today!"

Then she thought again about all the good things Mugisa was bringing. Mama said that soon Surprise would be sold for a lot of money. "It will be enough to tear down this old house," she had explained. "We will be able to put up a new one with a steel roof that won't leak during the rains."

Beatrice heard a rustle and noticed Bunane heading toward her with his empty milk pail. He eyed her new uniform and sighed. "You're so lucky. I wish *I* could go to school."

Beatrice reached out and touched Bunane's arm. "I've heard that your family is next in line to receive a goat."

A smile crossed Bunane's face. "Really?"

"Really."

Then Beatrice kissed Mugisa on the soft part of her nose, close to where her chin hairs curled just so, and started off to school.

Page and Lori's Story

AUTHOR

PAGE McBRIER was lucky enough to go to Uganda to meet Beatrice. She and Lori Lohstoeter had a six-hour drive to reach Beatrice's little village. After Page finished this story, she visited Beatrice again. By then, Beatrice had finished high school and was getting ready for college.

Other books by Page McBrier: *Oliver and the Lucky Duck* and *The Treehouse Times*

ILLUSTRATOR

LORI LOHSTOETER learned about Beatrice when she met someone from a special group that helps families. Lori wanted to draw the pictures for a book about Beatrice, but she needed to find someone to write the story. Lori asked Page, and they went to Africa to meet Beatrice and tell her story.

LOG ON Find out more about Page McBrier and Lori Lohstoeter at **www.macmillanmh.com**

FCAT Author's Purpose

Did Page McBrier want to entertain or inform her readers? Identify the author's purpose. Find details in the selection that support your answer.

FCAT Comprehension Check

Summarize

Use the Cause and Effect Chart to help you summarize *Beatrice's Goat*. Tell how and why Beatrice was finally able to go to school.

Cause	→	Effect
	→	
	→	
	→	

Think and Compare

READ
THINK
EXPLAIN

1. How does the goat help Beatrice earn money? Use story details to support your answer. **Make Inferences and Analyze: Cause and Effect**

READ
THINK
EXPLAIN

2. Reread page 194. At first, how does Beatrice feel about the **gift** of a goat? Why does she feel this way? Use information from the story in your answer. **Analyze**

3. Before you read this story, would you have thought a goat was a good gift? Why or why not? Did your opinion change after reading the story? Explain. **Evaluate**

4. Why is a goat a better gift than money for the people in Beatrice's village? Explain. **Synthesize**

5. Read "Helping People Help Themselves" on pages 186–187. How is this selection like *Beatrice's Goat*? How are the two selections different? Use details from both selections in your answer. **Reading/Writing Across Texts**

Social Studies

Genre

Newspaper Articles tell about important people and events and are part of daily or weekly newspapers.

FCAT Text Feature

Editorials are newspaper articles that present the opinions of the publisher or editors. They try to persuade the reader to do or believe something.

Content Vocabulary

achieve

determined

encourages

Ugandan Girl Reaches Goal

by Ann Frost

To Beatrice Biira, getting an education is the most important goal a person can have. Even when she was a little girl growing up in Uganda, she saw how important it is to get a good education. A goat named Mugisa helped her **achieve**, or reach, that goal.

After receiving Mugisa from the charity group Heifer International, Beatrice's family took care of the goat and the goat's young, which are called kids. With the money they made from selling milk and one of the kids, the Biiras were able to buy things they needed. Many people would have been satisfied with that, but Beatrice wanted more. She wanted to go to school.

Ten-year-old Beatrice had to start first grade with much younger students. This just made her more **determined** to work harder. Soon she caught up with her friends. Beatrice's good grades made it possible for her to go to school in the United States.

Even though it was hard for Beatrice to live so far away from her family, it has been worth it to her to get a good education.

Beatrice feeds Mugisa.

213

About Beatrice

Reading an Editorial

Editorials contain facts, as well as the opinions of the publisher or editors.

The News

| Vol. 3 | LATE CITY EDITION | April 17, 2007 |

> The title of a newspaper article or editorial is called the headline.

How Important Is Education? Ask Beatrice!

by Earl Clements, Jr.

> This tells an opinion.

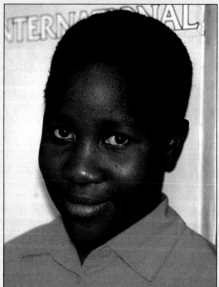

Getting an education should be one of the most important goals a person has. Beatrice Biira knew this when she was a little girl in Uganda. Beatrice's family could not buy the uniform and books she needed for school. When Heifer International gave her family a goat, Beatrice worked hard to take care of it and sell its milk. She earned enough money to buy books and a uniform. She worked hard at school and eventually went to college in the United States. Now Beatrice plans to help others get an education and a better life. Beatrice is an amazing young woman.

Education has changed Beatrice Biira's life. She has appeared on television to tell her story and has visited schools to talk about how Mugisa the goat changed her life.

Beatrice worked hard. She didn't give up. Today she **encourages**, or urges, students to read and help make the world a better place.

Beatrice visits classrooms to talk about her experiences.

 Connect and Compare

1. Which sentences in the editorial tell the writer's opinions? **Reading an Editorial**

2. How does the writer of the editorial feel about education? Do you agree or disagree? Explain. **Evaluate**

3. Think about this article and *Beatrice's Goat*. What information is the same in both selections? What facts do you learn from each? **Reading/Writing Across Texts**

 Social Studies Activity

Find out about an organization that helps people, such as Heifer International or Habitat for Humanity. Write an editorial that convinces people to donate money or time to that organization.

LOG ON Find out more about charitable organizations at **www.macmillanmh.com**

Writer's Craft

Transition Words

Good writers use **transition words** to connect ideas. Words such as *because, as a result, cause,* and *so* show causes and effects.

I used the word "so" to show cause and effect.

The phrase "As a result" explains what I did because of Bert's actions.

Write About Family

A Day with Bert

by Danielle L.

My baby brother Bert can be quite a handful. Last night I watched him while my mother made dinner. He gave me a hard time. First he threw his stuffed animals out of his crib and onto the floor. If I didn't give them back to him, he cried. So I brought him into my room. Because he loves to crawl, he knocked down my block castles and chewed on my books! As a result, I had to put my books on shelves and build new castles. Bert is a lot of work, but I am happy to be his big sister! I am hoping one day we will be able to play together.

Writing Prompt

Sometimes people have good stories to tell about family members.

Think of a story you have about a family member.

Now write a story about that family member.

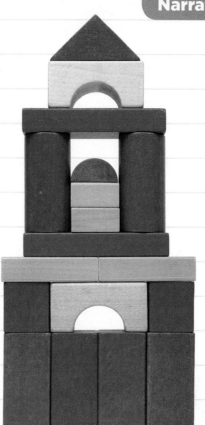

 FCAT Writer's Checklist

 Focus: My story is about someone in my family.

 Organization: I use **transition words** to show causes and effects.

✓ **Support:** All the details tell about my story.

 Conventions: I use subject and object pronouns correctly. All my words are spelled correctly.

Talk About It

How many different ways can people travel from one place to another?

 Find out more about movement and transportation at **www.macmillanmh.com**

IN MOTION

Visions of the Future from the Past

What opinions did experts have about movement and transportation throughout history? Take a look.

Lord Kelvin, a famous scientist, 1800s

Opinion: Airplanes will never fly.

Was he right? No. On December 17, 1903, the Wright brothers made the first controlled flight in a **powered** airplane.

Lee DeForest, a pioneer in radio, TV, and radar, 1900s

Opinion: No person will ever reach the moon.

Was he right? No. On July 20, 1969, Neil Armstrong stepped onto the moon and **declared**, "That's one small step for a man, one giant leap for mankind."

Jules Verne, science-fiction writer, in 1870

Opinion: People will be able to travel under water in airtight vessels.

Was he right?
Yes. Though

submarines already **existed**, it would be decades before they could stay submerged for long-distance travel.

Leonardo da Vinci, artist, scientist, inventor, 1400s

Opinion: People will fly in a machine with an overhead propeller.

Was he right?
Yes. This **artist's** sketch, made about 1490, shows a helicopter 400 years before its invention.

220

SMOOTH RIDING

This time line of inventions shows some real *movement!*

3800–3600 B.C.	The wheel
1783 A.D.	Hot air balloon Steamship
1831	Lawn mower
1885	Bicycle
1903	The Wright brothers' first flight
1908	Ford Model-T car
1939	Jet airplane
1980	In-line skates
1981	Space shuttle

LOG ON Find out more about transportation at www.macmillanmh.com

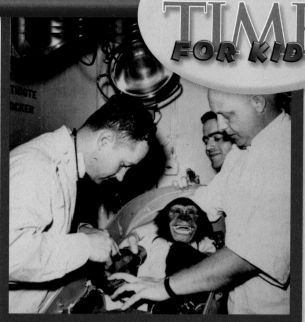

Where No Chimp Has Gone Before

On January 31, 1961, Ham the chimpanzee blasted off into space . . . and history books.

Ham's flight took him 156.5 miles into space at a speed of 5,800 miles per hour. The trip lasted 16.5 minutes. Then Ham's capsule splashed down into the Atlantic Ocean. Back on land, he gobbled up an apple and half an orange.

The U.S. space program took great pride in Ham. He paved the way for Alan Shepard to become the first American in space in May 1961.

After his space flight, Ham went on to live in a North Carolina zoo.

Comprehension

Genre

A **Nonfiction Article** gives information about a real person, place, or event.

Make Inferences and Analyze

FCAT Relevant Facts and Details
Facts and opinions are types of details that tell about a main idea. Facts can be proved. Opinions cannot.

A Carousel of Dreams

The creatures on the Children's Carousel at Riverbank State Park (above) were copied from kids' drawings, like the one below.

The carousel at Riverbank State Park in New York City is probably the most fantastic carousel in the country. It doesn't hold the usual herd of painted ponies. Instead, giant spiders pull a chariot, and a plaid zebra prances beside a two-headed octopus. These creatures were invented by kids. Milo Mottola, 32, is the artist who turned the kids' drawings into carousel critters.

Mottola believed kids should be a big part of his carousel project, so he held drawing classes in Riverbank State Park. The kids created more than 1,000 drawings of creatures. It was tough to choose only 32 of them for the carousel. "They were all my favorites!" Mottola **declared**.

When 9-year-old Grover Austin heads to the carousel, he hops on the green lion. He thinks it's the best because he created it! The **artist's** signature is carved on the floor beneath each animal. The original drawing hangs above it.

The Children's Carousel at Riverbank State Park is one of only 200 major carousels that remain today. Amusement parks and fairs now have faster rides. People today seem to prefer rides that are scarier or more exciting than the gentle carousels. But during the early 1900s, carousels were very popular. About 6,000 of them **existed** in the United States.

History in the Round

At one time, carousels were considered rides for adults, not kids. Most carousels were created by craftspeople who came to the United States from other countries. They had a lot of **pride** in their designs of fancy horses and chariots. Chariots are the carousel seats that are like benches or little carriages. Most of these old-style carousels are gone. Some were destroyed by fires and other disasters. Many were simply not taken care of. Some originals, however, are still standing and most likely are still making people happy. One of them is in San Diego, California. Another one is in Memphis, Tennessee.

Milo Mottola with some of the carousel's kid artists and their creations

The carousel that twirls in Seaport Village, San Diego, was built in 1895. The 41 hand-carved horses have natural horsehair tails. The 13 other animals include a giraffe, a dragon, a teddy bear, an elephant, a camel, a dog, and a lion. They were all made by hand, too. "This is one of the two best carousels in the entire nation," says Brad Perron. He's the owner of a company that fixes old carousels so they are like new again. "They don't make them this way anymore," says Perron. He's talking about animals carved by hand from wood. Newer carousel animals are usually made out of material that is mostly plastic. Some people think the old carousels were better than newer ones.

Riders of the Grand Carousel in Memphis, Tennessee, can choose to ride one of the 48 wooden horses or two hand-carved chariots. Built in 1909, the carousel spun its magic in Chicago, Illinois, for about ten years. Now it is a famous attraction in Tennessee's Libertyland Amusement Park. This carousel is one of a kind. It is so important that it is listed in the National Register of Historic Places.

The Grand Carousel in Memphis, Tennessee

These and other historic carousels are **powered** by a motor in the center of the ride. The motor is covered up by panels with pretty drawings and carvings on them. Older carousels even have mirrors and special music that blares from nearby speakers. Blinking, bright lights call riders to come take a spin.

Did You Know?

* The earliest known carousel in the U.S. appeared in Salem, Massachusetts, in 1799.

* Some historic carousel horses were made with brass rings so that people could try to grab on for a free ride.

* Usually, the fanciest and most decorated horses on a carousel are the ones facing the outside.

* Many original carousel horses built in the early 1900s had real horsehair.

* What's the difference between a carousel and a merry-go-round? Traditionally, carousels had only horses, but merry-go-rounds included other animals.

* Original wooden carousel horses today cost between $200 and $80,000 each.

FCAT
Think and Compare

1. Brad Perron says that the carousel at Seaport Village in San Diego is "one of the two best carousels in the entire nation." Is this statement a fact or an opinion? How do you know?

2. How were the creatures on the carousel at Riverbank State Park created?

3. Would you rather ride a carousel or a faster, scarier ride at an amusement park? Why?

4. Compare the motion of the space capsule that Ham the chimpanzee rode with the motion of a carousel.

FCAT Test Strategy

Author and Me

The answer is not directly stated. Think about what you have read to figure out the best answer.

Bikes in sharing programs are usually painted a bright color, such as red, yellow, or orange.

GETTING A FREE RIDE

Suppose you find a bright yellow bike on a street corner in the city. You hop on and pedal away. But wait—isn't this stealing? No one yells, "Stop! Thief!" That's because this free ride is just fine with the city.

In 1994 a group of people got together in Portland, Oregon. Their goal was to improve the quality of life in their city. They wanted to provide free transportation and help stop pollution. A local recycling center agreed to donate 10 used bikes. The group painted the bikes bright yellow, put up signs about the free rides, and the Yellow Bike Project was born.

Television and newspapers around the country liked the Yellow Bike Project's story. Other cities realized they needed to get citizens out of their cars and onto pollution-free bikes, too. Soon, similar bike programs were set up in cities in six other states. Hundreds of free bikes were now available in U.S. cities such as Austin, Texas, and St. Paul, Minnesota. People everywhere were biking to work, to school, to sightsee, or to run errands.

Today, wonderful bike-sharing projects exist across the world. Does bike sharing always work? Sometimes people steal bikes, but most obey the rules. What would be the point of stealing something that's free?

226

Go on ▶

1 Why was the Yellow Bike Project started?

(A) to sell more bicycles in cities

(B) to teach bicycle safety and rules in cities

(C) to teach people who don't have a bicycle how to ride

(D) to help control pollution by reducing the use of cars

2 Why are the bicycles used in this program and similar programs painted bright colors?

(F) so the bikes are the same color as taxi cabs

(G) so the bikes will stand out and be noticed

(H) so people will know what city they are in

(I) so other cyclists will know who to follow

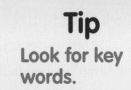

Tip
Look for key words.

3 Why did the author write "Getting a Free Ride"?

(A) to describe the various types of bikes available to riders

(B) to persuade local bicycle shops to donate to similar programs

(C) to convince other cities that they should have a bike sharing program

(D) to inform people about the Yellow Bike Project and other bike sharing programs

4 READ THINK EXPLAIN
How does the author feel about the bike sharing program? What facts and opinions in the article help you figure this out?

5 READ THINK EXPLAIN
Planning for the bike project in Oregon began in 1994. Using details in the article, describe each step the group in Oregon took to get the Yellow Bike Project running.

Write to a Prompt

FCAT People often enjoy games and rides.

Think about a time you enjoyed a game or ride.

Now <u>write a story about</u> the time you enjoyed a game or ride.

> Narrative writing tells a story about a personal or fictional experience.

> To figure out if a writing prompt asks for narrative writing, look for clue words, such as <u>write a story about</u> or <u>tell what happened</u>.

Below see how one student begins a response to the prompt above.

> The story events are told in a sequence that makes sense.

I gave my blue ticket to the man and ran to the horse I had chosen. I climbed up and held the gold pole with both hands. Loud music started, and the carousel began to turn.

My beautiful horse galloped up and down. The purple-gray mane looked like it was waving in the air. My saddle was painted bright red and yellow. The horse was grayish with smoky black spots. It was the best horse on the carousel!

When the ride stopped, I looked at the other people. A little kid about 2 years old had started to cry. A grandma sat on a bench with a baby on her lap. The baby's eyes were really big! Some big kids looked disappointed that the ride was over.

Writing Prompt

Respond in writing to the prompt below. Before you write, read the Writing Hints for Prompts. Remember to review the hints after you finish writing.

FCAT

Most students like to play in the playground or park. Think of a time when you played in the playground or park. Now write a story about a time you played in the playground or park.

Writing Hints for Prompts

- ☑ Read the prompt carefully.
- ☑ Plan your writing by organizing your ideas.
- ☑ Support your ideas by telling more about each event.
- ☑ Use a variety of sentence structures.
- ☑ Choose words that help others understand what you mean.
- ☑ Review and edit your writing.

229

Talk About It

A hero is any person who helps others. What qualities do all heroes have?

LOG ON Find out more about heroes at **www.macmillanmh.com**

HEROES

To the Rescue

by Daniel Dahari

It was recess time. It was a perfect spring day, and Ms. Clark's class hurried outdoors.

Erica headed straight for the slide. There was nothing better than a climb and a slide. Especially on a day like this! She was just about to place her foot on the ladder when she stopped and **screamed** with fear. Everyone ran over to find out what had happened. Erica stood there, **numb**. She couldn't move an inch. Under the ladder's first rung was a turtle, a big turtle—and it was stuck!

"Stand clear," warned Ms. Clark. "It's trying to **escape**, but it can't get out. Poor thing."

Several boys and girls **fled** across the yard. That turtle looked mean.

"That's a snapping turtle," said Jeff. "Snappers have really strong jaws. That thing can really bite! I wonder how it got here."

The turtle tried to dig with its feet but remained stuck.

"I'll call the police," said Ms. Clark. "They'll send over Animal Control. They'll know what to do."

An Animal Control van pulled up and **shuddered** to a stop. The officer said, "That's a snapping turtle, all right. It must have come up from the marsh. We'd better get him back where he belongs."

She got a small shovel and carefully removed the sand beneath the turtle. Then the officer gently wrapped the turtle in a towel. She said, "You did the right thing by calling me. It's very dangerous to try to free a trapped animal yourselves."

Ms. Clark took a picture. "This **image** will go on the front page of the school **newspaper** next week," she said. "It's not every day that we get a snapshot of a snapping turtle!"

Reread for Comprehension

Make Inferences and Analyze

FCAT **Plot Development** To better understand the characters' actions and story events, good readers **make predictions**. A prediction tells about what will happen next in the story. To make a prediction, use story clues and what you know.

Reread the selection. Use your Predictions Chart to record a prediction. Then confirm your prediction. Record **what happens**.

What I Predict	What Happens

Comprehension

Genre

Realistic Fiction is an invented story that could have happened in real life.

Make Inferences and Analyze

FCAT **Plot Development**

As you read, use your Predictions Chart.

What I Predict	What Happens

Read to Find Out

How does the printer help the workers at the plant?

THE PRINTER

by Myron Uhlberg
illustrated by Henri Sørensen

My father was a printer. He wore a printer's four-cornered **newspaper** hat. Every day after work, he brought home the next day's paper. After reading it, he always folded a page into a small hat and gently placed it on my head.

I would not take off my newspaper hat until bedtime.

My father was deaf. Though he could not hear, he felt through the soles of his shoes the pounding and rumbling of the giant printing presses that daily spat out the newspaper he helped create.

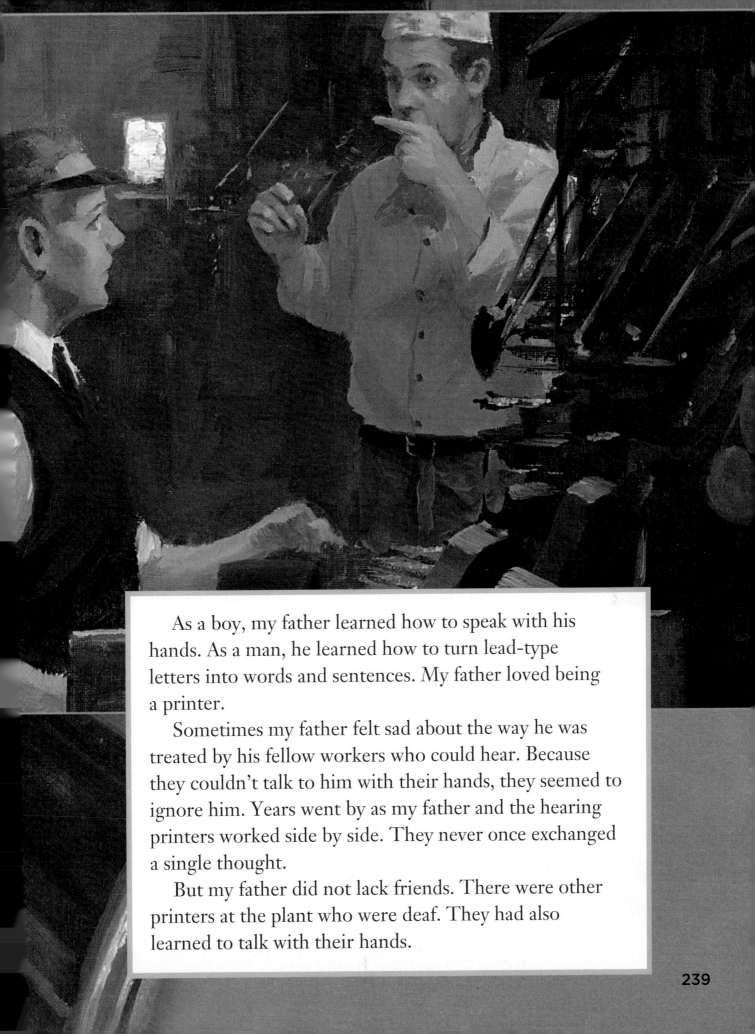

As a boy, my father learned how to speak with his hands. As a man, he learned how to turn lead-type letters into words and sentences. My father loved being a printer.

Sometimes my father felt sad about the way he was treated by his fellow workers who could hear. Because they couldn't talk to him with their hands, they seemed to ignore him. Years went by as my father and the hearing printers worked side by side. They never once exchanged a single thought.

But my father did not lack friends. There were other printers at the plant who were deaf. They had also learned to talk with their hands.

One day, while the giant presses ran, their noises shutting out all other sound, my father spotted a fire flickering in a far corner of the pressroom.

The fire was spreading quickly, silently. Suddenly, the wood floor burst into flames.

My father knew he had to tell everyone. He couldn't speak to shout a warning. Even if he could, no one would hear him over the loud roar of the presses.

But he could speak with his hands.

FCAT Plot Development

How will the printer tell the other workers about the fire?

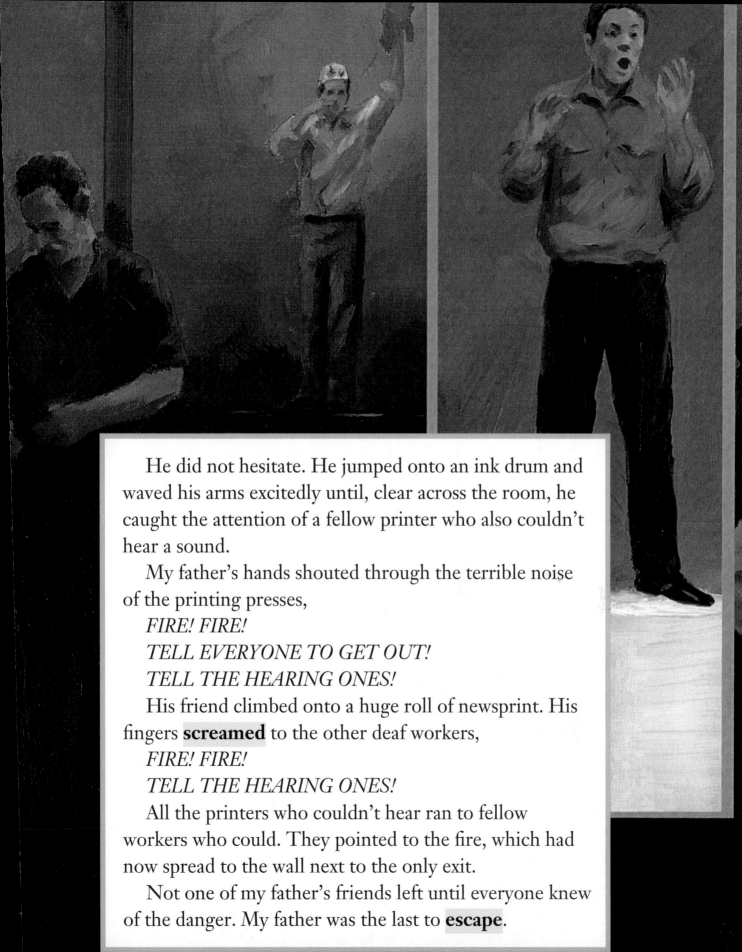

He did not hesitate. He jumped onto an ink drum and waved his arms excitedly until, clear across the room, he caught the attention of a fellow printer who also couldn't hear a sound.

My father's hands shouted through the terrible noise of the printing presses,

FIRE! FIRE!

TELL EVERYONE TO GET OUT!

TELL THE HEARING ONES!

His friend climbed onto a huge roll of newsprint. His fingers **screamed** to the other deaf workers,

FIRE! FIRE!

TELL THE HEARING ONES!

All the printers who couldn't hear ran to fellow workers who could. They pointed to the fire, which had now spread to the wall next to the only exit.

Not one of my father's friends left until everyone knew of the danger. My father was the last to **escape**.

By the time everyone had **fled**, the fire—feeding on huge quantities of paper—had engulfed the enormous plant. The giant presses, some still spewing out burning sheets of newspaper, had fallen partly through the floor. Great shafts of flame shot out of the bursting windows.

The printers stood in the street, broken glass at their feet. They embraced one another as the fire engines arrived. They were happy to be alive.

My father stood alone, struck **numb** by the last **image** of the burning presses.

The fire destroyed the printing presses. The plant had to close for repairs. But not one printer had been hurt.

When the printing plant finally reopened, my father went back to the work he loved. The new presses were switched on and roared into life.

FCAT Plot Development

How will the other printers treat the narrator's father now that the plant has reopened?

247

When the day's newspaper had been printed, the presses **shuddered** to a stop. Now there was silence.

In the midst of the stillness, my father's co-workers gathered around him. They presented him with a hat made of the freshly printed newspaper.

And as my father put the hat on his head, all the printers who could hear did something surprising.

They told him THANK YOU with their hands.

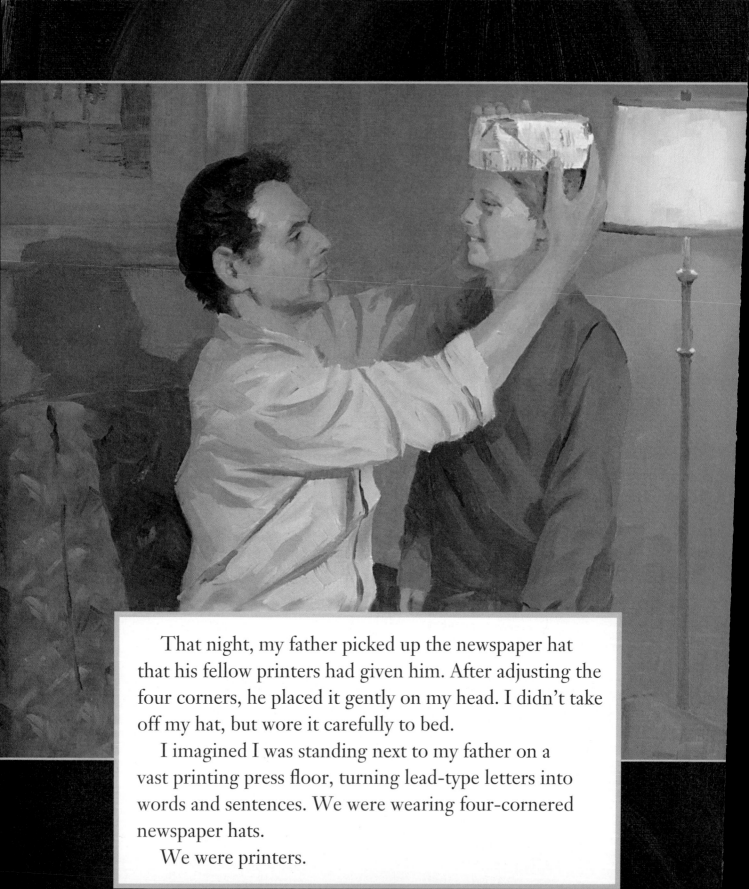

That night, my father picked up the newspaper hat that his fellow printers had given him. After adjusting the four corners, he placed it gently on my head. I didn't take off my hat, but wore it carefully to bed.

I imagined I was standing next to my father on a vast printing press floor, turning lead-type letters into words and sentences. We were wearing four-cornered newspaper hats.

We were printers.

251

SAVE THE DAY WITH MYRON AND HENRI

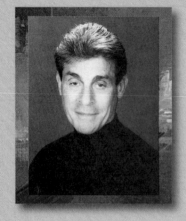

Author

Myron Uhlberg used memories of his father to write his story. Myron's father was born deaf. He worked as a newspaper printer just like the father in the story. When Myron was young, he would visit his father at work. Even today, Myron still remembers how noisy the pressroom was. He also remembers the hats his father made out of newspaper for him.

Other books by Myron Uhlberg:
Flying Over Brooklyn and *Mad Dog McGraw*

Illustrator

Henri Sørensen grew up in Denmark and spent much of his childhood in a quiet museum. Every week he visited the museum to look at paintings. When Henri illustrates a story, he thinks about how the words make him feel. Then he tries to show the feeling in his pictures.

Find out more about Myron Uhlberg and Henri Sørensen at
www.macmillanmh.com

FCAT Author's Purpose

What was Myron Uhlberg's purpose in writing this selection? Use details from *The Printer* to support your answer.

FCAT Comprehension Check

Summarize

Use your Predictions Chart to help summarize what happens in *The Printer*. Tell what you thought would happen and what really happened at the end of the story.

What I Predict	What Happens

Think and Compare

1. What clues can you use to predict the printer's actions after he notices the fire in the **newspaper** plant? Use story details in your answer. **Make Inferences and Analyze: Plot Development**

2. Reread page 248. How do the hearing printers show that they have changed? Use details from the story in your answer. **Evaluate**

3. What are some good reasons for people to learn sign language? **Synthesize**

4. What lesson does the writer want people to learn from this story? How do you know? **Analyze**

5. Read "To the Rescue" on pages 232–233. How are the warning and rescue in this story different from the warning and rescue in *The Printer*? Use details from both selections in your answer. **Reading/Writing Across Texts**

SOUND IS ENERGY!

by Vivian Pham

What Is Energy?

You hear about energy all the time. You turn off lights to save energy. You eat food so that you can have energy to do things. Energy is the ability to do work. Energy is all around us. Heat, light, and sound are kinds of energy. Energy from heat is used by your stove. Energy from light can light your home. Energy from sound can be music to your ears.

Heat is the energy used to fry an egg.

A rock dropped into a puddle can produce ripples as shown above.

When someone plays a saxophone, air vibrates inside of it. Touch the instrument and you can feel it vibrate.

How Does Energy Travel?

Energy travels in **waves**. Think about throwing a stone into a pond. The stone creates waves in the water. The waves spread out from where the stone hits the water. The waves are like **vibrations** in the water. A vibration is when something moves up and down or side to side. You can see vibrations when you pluck a guitar string. You can feel vibrations when you place your fingers on your throat as you talk.

What Makes Sound?

When something vibrates, it causes sound waves. Sound is made from vibrations. If something vibrates quickly it makes a high sound. If something vibrates slowly it makes a low sound. **Pitch** is how high or low a sound is. Sound can travel through air and water. Sound can also travel through objects. If you put your ear on your desk and tap on it, you will hear sound.

Sound is made when you strum the strings of a guitar.

How Do We Hear?

Sound waves travel from an object to your ears. Your ears are made to hear the sound vibrations around you. Sound waves go through your ear canal and cause your eardrum to vibrate. When your eardrum vibrates, three tiny bones in your ear move. These bones are called the malleous (hammer), incus (anvil), and stapes (stirrup). The three bones send vibrations to the cochlea. The cochlea has many tiny hairs that send signals to your brain. You brain reads these signals, and you understand what you hear.

Hearing aids help people who hear poorly. A hearing aid makes sounds louder.

THE PARTS OF THE EAR

Reading a Diagram
Look at this diagram to see where the parts of the ear are located.

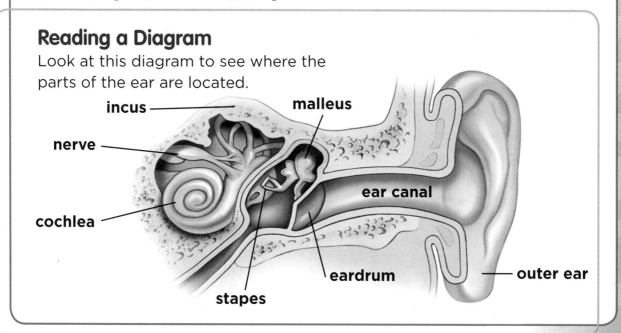

incus — malleus — ear canal — outer ear — eardrum — stapes — cochlea — nerve

FCAT Connect and Compare

1. Look at the diagram. Describe where sound waves go when they enter your ear. **Reading a Diagram**

2. What is a vibration? What do vibrations have to do with sound? **Apply**

3. Use the information in this article. Explain how the father in *The Printer* could feel the pounding and rumbling of the printing presses through his shoes. **Reading/Writing Across Texts**

Science Activity

Many animals, such as rabbits or elephants, have unusually large ears. Other animals, such as moths and bats, use different types of hearing than humans. Research an animal to see how it hears. Then draw and label the important parts of the animal's hearing system.

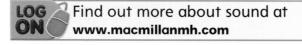

LOG ON Find out more about sound at www.macmillanmh.com

Write an Introductory Speech

Writer's Craft

FCAT Facts and Opinions

Facts and opinions are kinds of details that writers use to persuade. A fact is something that can be proved. An opinion tells what the writer thinks.

I began by telling my opinion of my teacher.

I included facts to support my opinions.

Meet Mrs. Adorno

by Edward M.

Today we are giving the award for favorite teacher to Mrs. Adorno. She is the nicest, funniest teacher I have ever had. A lot of you must think so too, because you voted for her. She makes science seem like fun. After school she gives students extra help if we have problems understanding something. Mrs. Adorno always makes us laugh with her stories. Also, she is our softball team's biggest fan. This year she came to all of our games and cheered for us! Now say hello to our favorite teacher, Mrs. Adorno!

258

Writing Prompt

People often know a special person whom they really like.

Think about a person you really like.

Now write an introductory speech to explain why you like this person.

 **Writer's Checklist**

 Focus: My writing has a central idea.

 Organization: I begin with a topic sentence.

 Support: I use **facts and opinions** to tell about my person.

 Conventions: My pronouns and verbs agree. All my words are spelled correctly.

Talk About It

How are animals' homes
similar to people's homes?

LOG ON Find out more about
animal homes at
www.macmillanmh.com

ANiMAL
ARCHITECTS

Web Spinners

by Steven Kutner

Just as bees build **hives** to live in, spiders spin webs. Spiders are talented **architects**. They design and build **structures** to live in that are works of art. These structures are also traps for other insects.

Spinning Silk

Spider webs are made from silk. Spiders make silk in their bellies. Their silk-making gland has many tiny holes. The silk goes through the holes to get outside the spider's body. When it meets the air, the silk forms a thread. The thread is very thin but very strong.

Spiders can make different kinds of silk. Some **contain** a material that makes the silk sticky. Other silks do not have this material.

A spider spins a thread behind itself everywhere it goes. This thread is called a dragline. If an enemy comes near, the spider **retreats** on its dragline. Being able to go backward on its own line is like having a self-made escape route!

Tangled Webs

Different spiders build different kinds of webs. The simplest web is called a tangled web. It is just a mess of threads that are attached to something. A cobweb is a dusty, old, tangled web.

Cellar Spiders

Some spiders are called cellar spiders. This is because they usually build tangled webs in cellars or other dark places.

Orb Weavers

The most common webs are shaped like wheels. They are built by orb weavers. You can find these webs in open areas, such as the spaces between branches.

Water Spiders

The water spider builds its web in tiny ponds and other places with **shallow** water. The web looks like a small air-filled balloon. The water spider feeds and raises its family inside this cozy **shelter**.

Reread for **Comprehension**

Summarize

FCAT Relevant Facts and Details In some nonfiction articles, authors use **relevant facts and details** to describe the **main ideas** of a topic. This is called the description text structure. Nonfiction is easy to summarize when it is organized in this way.

Reread the selection. Use your Description Web to record the details about one description example.

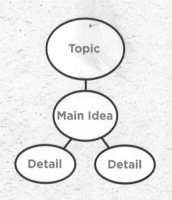

Topic

Main Idea

Detail   Detail

Comprehension

Genre
Informational Nonfiction is a detailed explanation of real things using facts.

Summarize
Relevant Facts and Details

As you read, use your Description Web.

Topic

Main Idea

Detail   Detail

Read to Find Out
How are some animal homes similar to your home?

Animal Homes

by Ann O. Squire

Why Do Animals Need Homes?

Animals need homes for many of the same reasons that people do. What are some of those reasons? Start by thinking about your own home, and the kinds of things you do there.

Some kinds of penguins build nests to protect their chicks.

Eating is one very important thing you do every day. Your house has a kitchen where you store and prepare food. Some animals also keep food in their homes. Honeybees, for example, live in **hives** made up of waxy honeycombs. Each honeycomb has many six-sided cubbies, or cells, where the bees store their honey.

The cells of the honeycomb are also used as nurseries for young bees. And that may remind you of another reason people and animals need homes. They need a safe place to raise their young. Birds' nests, alligator mounds, and the dens of polar bears are other kinds of homes made for raising a family.

FCAT **Relevant Facts and Details**

What are two ways honeybees use their hives?

▲ Other cells are used as nurseries for bee larvae.

Bees store honey in some ▶ of the cells of their hive.

A desert tortoise in its burrow

Doesn't it feel good to come indoors on a cold winter day or turn up the air conditioner on a hot and humid summer night? That's another reason we need a home—to protect us from bad weather.

The desert tortoise lives in dry parts of the southwestern United States, where summer temperatures often go above 100 degrees Fahrenheit (38 degrees Celsius). To escape the heat, the tortoise digs a **shallow** burrow, or hole, where it can rest during the hottest part of the day.

In the winter, when temperatures fall below freezing, the tortoise digs a much deeper burrow. Then it climbs in and spends the winter there, hibernating with other tortoises.

Underground burrows also give animals a place to hide from their enemies. Prairie dogs, for example, dig long, winding burrows with many different rooms and tunnels.

Many people's homes have a front door, a back door, and maybe even a side door. A prairie-dog burrow has several openings, too. If a hungry predator invades the burrow through the main entrance, the prairie dogs can escape out the back way.

FCAT Relevant Facts and Details
Use facts and details to describe a prairie-dog burrow.

A prairie dog standing near its burrow entrance

A coyote trying to invade a prairie-dog burrow

Some animals build homes for more tricky reasons. Many spiders spin webs mainly to trap unlucky insects.

Now that you know some of the reasons animals need homes, let's find out about some unusual animal homes.

A weaverbird
building its nest

Building a Home

Many animals build their own homes. These animal **architects** can be birds, mammals, insects, and even fish.

The African weaverbird's name is a clue to the way this bird builds its nest. The male weaverbird gathers long blades of grass, which he knots and weaves into a sturdy ring. Then he adds grass to the ring, making a hollow ball. To keep out tree snakes, the ball is open only at the bottom. When the nest is finished, the weaverbird calls to attract nearby females. If a female likes the nest, she moves in, and the two raise a family.

◄ A spider trapping prey in its web

Termite towers have many rooms.

Some insects build homes, too. One of the largest and most complicated **structures** in the animal world is created by tiny African termites.

A termite tower may be as tall as a giraffe and **contain** millions of termites. The walls of the tower are made of a rock-hard mixture of dirt and saliva. They contain air shafts that keep the inside of the tower cool, even in the blazing sun.

The tower has many special rooms. It has a royal chamber, where the termite king and queen live, nurseries for the young, rooms for storing food, and even an underground garden. Most termites live for only a few years, but a termite tower may last for close to a century.

A termite tower in Ghana, Africa

Beavers use sticks and mud to build a dam. Then they build their lodge in the middle of the pond formed by the dam.

Have you ever heard people say someone is as "busy as a beaver"? You'd know what they mean if you saw how much work goes into building a beaver lodge.

First, the beavers use sticks and mud to make a dam across a stream. Then water backs up behind the dam to form a pond. In the center of the pond, the beavers build their lodge. It looks like nothing more than a pile of sticks, but the lodge has a room inside that is reached by underwater tunnels. The beavers can come and go easily, but it's almost impossible for wolves and other predators to find a way in.

The hermit crab makes its home in an empty seashell.

Finding a Home

Bees, weaverbirds, termites, and beavers all work long and hard to build their homes. But some animals take the easy way out. They look around for ready-made lodgings.

Unlike most other crabs, the hermit crab does not have a hard shell to protect it. It needs a safe place to live, so the hermit crab searches for an empty snail shell. When it finds a shell that fits, the hermit crab squeezes inside. It stays there until it grows too big for that shell. Then it must look for a larger shell.

The pea crab doesn't even wait until a shell is empty. This tiny crab moves in with the original owner! It squeezes into the shell of a mussel, clam, or oyster while that animal is still alive. The shellfish isn't even bothered by the pea crab sharing its home. As the shellfish filters food through its gills, the pea crab catches tiny bits of food as they float past.

A pea crab

A white cowbird egg in a nest containing blue wood thrush eggs

A cowbird chick being raised by a yellow warbler

The cowbird is even more daring. Instead of building its own nest, the female cowbird searches the forest for other nesting birds. When she sees a likely couple, she settles down to wait.

As soon as the unsuspecting birds leave their nest, the cowbird darts in and throws out one of their eggs. Then she quickly lays one of her own. The nesting birds never know the difference! They raise the cowbird chick as if it were one of their own.

Burrowing owls ▶

Birds don't usually live underground, but one that does is the burrowing owl. These long-legged owls sometimes move into abandoned prairie-dog burrows. The birds come out in the cool of the evening to hunt small rodents, frogs, and insects.

Mobile Homes

A turtle can protect itself by retreating into its shell.

Most people and most animals live in homes that stay in one place. But if you've ever traveled in a camper, trailer or boat, you know that some kinds of homes can move around with you. Did you know that some animals also live in "mobile homes"?

Tortoises and turtles move slowly. You might think they would be easy prey for any animal that wanted to eat them. But tortoises and turtles can escape into the safety of their homes in a flash, simply by pulling their head and feet inside their hard shell.

**Turtles sunning themselves
on a log**

The snail is another animal that carries its house on its back. Snails need damp conditions in order to survive. In cold or dry weather, the snail **retreats** into its spiral shell to avoid drying out.

Like turtles, snails can retreat into their shells.

A kind of caterpillar called the bagworm makes its home out of twigs woven together with silk. The bagworm lives inside this silken case and drags its **shelter** along as it moves from branch to branch feeding on leaves.

A bagworm hanging from a spruce tree

At Home with Ann

AUTHOR
Ann O. Squire

is an expert on how animals behave. Before Ann began to write books for children, she studied many different kinds of animals. She has studied everything from rats to the African electric fish.

Other books by Ann O. Squire: *Growing Crystals* and *Seashells*

LOG ON Find out more about Ann O. Squire at **www.macmillanmh.com**

FCAT Author's Purpose

Nonfiction authors often write to inform or explain. Why did Ann O. Squire write *Animal Homes*? What are some details that help you figure out her purpose?

FCAT Comprehension Check

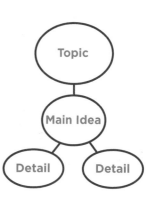

Summarize

Use the Description Web to help you summarize facts about *Animal Homes.* Create a topic sentence about animal homes. Then describe the main ideas using important information about different animal homes.

Topic

Main Idea

Detail   Detail

Think and Compare

1. Choose an animal that carries its **shelter** around. Using details from the text and your Description Web, describe that animal and its home. **Summarize: Relevant Facts and Details**

2. Reread pages 278–279 of *Animal Homes.* Describe mobile homes and the animals that live in them. How is a mobile home more useful than a nest or web? Use story details in your answer. **Analyze**

3. Which animal home in this story would you like to learn more about? Explain your answer. **Synthesize**

4. Why is studying animal homes important for people? **Evaluate**

5. Read "Web Spinners" on pages 262–263. Look at the photographs in the two selections you have read. Compare the structures of the spider webs with the structure of another animal home. Use details from both selections in your answer. **Reading/Writing Across Texts**

Home Sweet Home

FCAT

Poetry

A **Limerick** is a short funny poem. It has five lines. Usually the last words in the first, second, and fifth lines rhyme. The third and fourth lines usually rhyme with each other.

Literary Elements

A **Simile** compares two different things by using the word *like* or *as*.

A **Rhythmic Pattern** is a beat created by a pattern of stressed and unstressed syllables.

A flea on a pooch doesn't care

Which part it is crossing to where.

  Like mud to a frog

  Any part of a dog

Suits a flea, and it's glad to be there.

— *John Ciardi*

The rhythmic pattern of these two lines creates the beat: da DAH da da DAH da da DAH.

282

Limerick

Think of darkness. Then think of the mole

In his tunnel: black, black as coal. ◄

But the traffic is light,

And the weather's all right,

And the tunnel is free—there's no toll.

— *David McCord*

> This simile compares two unlike things: the darkness of the tunnel and coal.

FCAT Connect and Compare

1. In the second limerick, what picture comes to mind when you read the simile "black as coal"? **Simile**

2. Reread the first two lines of "Home Sweet Home." Compare the rhythmic patterns in these lines. **Evaluate**

3. Which animals in *Animal Homes* have homes similar to a mole's? How are they alike? **Reading/Writing Across Texts**

 Find out more about limericks at
www.macmillanmh.com

Write a Descriptive Poem

I wrote a simile to compare lizards to rabbits.

I used descriptive words to describe how a turtle moves.

Turtles Don't Hurry

by Sam C.

Turtles are reptiles,
As everyone knows.
They're cold-blooded,
And they have feet and tiny toes.
While lizards are quick,
Like rabbits with scales,
Turtles don't hurry.
They move slowly like snails.
They'll never leap up,
Or jump out or attack.
You'd move slowly, too,
With a house on your back!

Writing Prompt

People often write poems about animals.

Think about an animal you would like to write a descriptive poem about.

Now write a descriptive poem about that animal.

FCAT Writer's Checklist

 Focus: I write about one clear topic.

 Organization: All the details tell about the topic.

 Support: I use **figurative language**, such as similes and descriptive words.

 Conventions: I use pronoun contractions correctly. All my words are spelled correctly.

FCAT **Review**

Cause and Effect
Chronological Order
Plot Development
Context Clues
Compound Words
Charts

Nancy's Library

Nancy was upset. She used to love going to the library across the street. Now nobody wanted to go there anymore. The building needed to be repainted. The lawn and sidewalk out front were full of garbage.

What could she do? Nancy's mother encouraged her to think about how they could help. "Try making a list," suggested her mother.

Nancy took a long time writing all of her ideas. Her mother came in to check on her.

"Well," Nancy said, "we could call the town offices to see if they could help us clean the trash. We could see if they have people who paint. What do you think, Mom?"

"I think those are great ideas!" said Nancy's mother. When they contacted the town office, they learned that the money for libraries had been cut. The people at the town park offices suggested that Nancy organize a neighborhood cleanup.

Nancy's mother promised to help her plan the cleanup.

"Okay," Nancy said, "let's make a list of what we'll need."

"First," Nancy's mother replied, "we'll need lots of big trash bags for trash."

Nancy added, "And paint. Plus we have to choose a date for the cleanup and make signs to get people to come."

Soon the big day arrived. Nancy had contacted all of her friends, and they were there at the library. Some of their parents were there, too. Within a couple of hours, six trash bags were filled. The grass was almost clean! Some parents repainted the door, walls, and railings. The whole area looked much better. Nancy felt proud.

"But how will we keep it this way?" Nancy asked her mother.

"Why not ask everybody else for ideas this time," suggested her mother.

Nancy asked her friends and their families. She was amazed at what they had to say. Nearly all of them said that they would come again to do another cleanup. "We need this library," said one dad. "You kids should have a safe, clean place to read and study."

"Plus, the lawn is a great place for story hour," said one of the moms. "Let's try to keep it nice."

"Thank you so much!" cried Nancy.

"No, thank *you*," said Nancy's mother. "You're the one who got us moving and gave us back our library!"

TORNADOES

Nature's Toughest Storms

What Is a Tornado?

A tornado is a funnel of wind spinning very fast. Its wind can blow as fast as 300 miles per hour, which is almost six times the speed limit on a highway! Tornadoes can be caused by powerful thunderstorms called supercells. Cold, dry air mixing with warm, moist air makes a supercell. When the warm air in the supercell rises very quickly, it starts to spin into a tornado.

When a tornado reaches the ground, it begins to travel. A tornado can have a straight, a zigzag, or a circular path. The damage along this path can be as wide as 1 or 2 miles and as long as 50 miles. Tornadoes typically touch down for only two or three minutes.

At first a tornado's long cone shape is almost invisible. As it picks up dirt and other materials, the tornado gets darker and becomes easier to see. A tornado can also pick up cars, trees, and parts of buildings.

Staying Safe in a Tornado

Tornadoes are hard to predict, but meteorologists can help with this. Be sure to listen to local weather warnings. Also, the sky might appear slightly greenish just before a tornado. Loud winds that sound like a train might mean a tornado is very close.

The best place to take cover from a tornado is in a place without windows, such as a cellar, hallway, or closet. People in cars should stop driving and get into a building as quickly as possible.

Tornadoes come in different shapes and sizes.

The Fujita Pearson TORNADO Scale

F-Scale Number	Intensity	Wind Speed	Amount of Damage Done
F0	Gale	40-72 mph	It can break tree branches and damage chimneys.
F1	Moderate	73-112 mph	It can damage roofs and overturn mobile homes.
F2	Significant	113-157 mph	It can pick up trees and damage houses.
F3	Severe	158-206 mph	It can destroy house roofs and walls, move cars, and overturn trains.
F4	Devastating	207-260 mph	It can knock down even strong walls in big buildings.
F5	Incredible	261-318 mph	It can lift up and carry houses.

Talk About It

Neighbors often like to help each other. How do you help your neighbors?

LOG ON Find out more about helping neighbors at
www.macmillanmh.com

Helping
Our
Neighbors

291

What Should I Be?

by Carol R.

When I walk around my neighborhood, I see people working to protect and help me and my family. Firefighters, letter carriers, and police officers are community workers. They make my neighborhood a better place to live. When I am older, I would like to be a community worker, but which job should I choose?

Letter Carriers

Letter carriers deliver our mail and drop off packages and magazines. They work in every town and city in the United States.

The letter carrier in my neighborhood is Mr. Vasquez. He works **downtown**, walking from block to block to deliver mail to each address along the route. He doesn't carry big boxes, like the ones that hold stoves and washing machines. Trucks deliver **appliances** like those! Maybe I will be a letter carrier.

Police Officers

Police officers, like Officer Morena, keep us safe. Home and business **owners** depend on the police to guard our families, our property, and our streets.

Police may also work at sites where the **construction** of new buildings takes place. They direct traffic to keep the workers and drivers safe. Officer Morena can find lost people and help if there is an accident. She has special **equipment**, such as a two-way radio, so she can talk to other officers. Being a police officer might be a good job.

Firefighters

Firefighters are brave, like Chief Cole. They risk their lives to save people caught in fires. They also check smoke alarms in schools, as well as fire hydrants along the road to make sure they are tightly sealed. **Leaky** hydrants may not have enough water when the time comes to fight a fire.

Chief Cole is a good firefighter. Maybe I will be one too, someday.

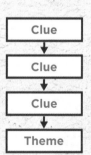

Reread for Comprehension

FCAT

Analyze Story Structure

Essential Message/Theme An essential message is what an author wants you to learn from a story or article. The essential message is also called the **theme**. An article or story's theme is usually not stated. To find the theme, think about the story structure. Think about the characters' actions and how the story ends.

Reread the selection. Use your Theme Map to record **clues** that help you figure out the article's theme.

| Clue |
| Clue |
| Clue |
| Theme |

Comprehension

Genre

Realistic Fiction is an invented story that could have happened in real life.

Analyze Story Structure

Essential Message/Theme

As you read, use your Theme Map.

```
Clue
  ↓
Clue
  ↓
Clue
  ↓
Theme
```

Read to Find Out

What is the essential message, or theme, of this story?

A Castle on Viola Street

by DyAnne DiSalvo

Award
Winning
Author

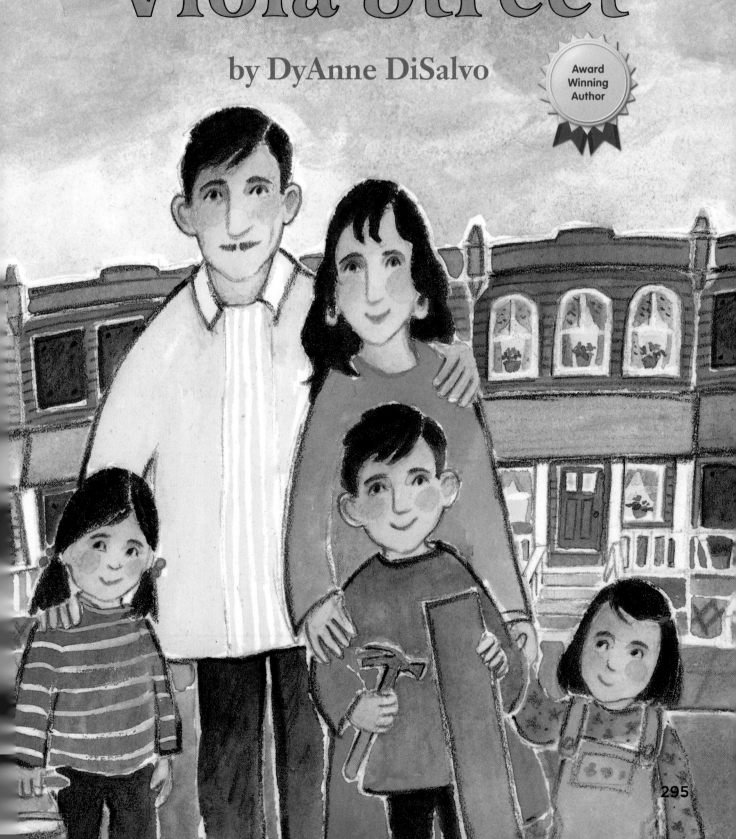

In the old days, before I was ten, we rented an apartment on Emerald Street. It was a small place to live in for one whole family, but somehow we made the room.

There always seemed to be enough to go around, even with five people at our table.

Every morning my father would get up even before the sun. "Someday things will change around here," he would whisper to me. He usually said this during the winter when the house was beginning to feel chilly. Then he'd kiss us good-bye, tuck up our blankets, and leave for his job at the diner.

My mother worked part-time in the **downtown** bakery while my sisters and I were at school. After school she'd sit on the stoop and watch us play.

Sometimes my mother would flip through a magazine. She'd show me pictures of houses with gardens and porches. They all looked like castles to me. I'd puff out my cheeks when I looked at our place. It was old and peeling and sorry.

That's when my mother would hug me and say, "Our family is rich in more ways than we can count."

FCAT **Essential Message/Theme**
Why does the mother look at pictures of houses?

On Saturday mornings my mother would weigh my pockets down with quarters for the Laundromat.

"Hold Andy's hand," she'd tell my sister.

Then my mother would slip two brown-bagged lunches in the wagon with a dollar for a treat. My sister and I would bump our cart to the Soap & Go on Viola Street.

Now, across the street from the Soap & Go were three boarded-up houses. My father said it was a shame. "Somebody should do something about that," he'd say whenever he saw them. So when a truck pulled up and workers unloaded **equipment**, I started to pay attention.

"What's going on over there?" a lady at the Soap &
Go asked.

Mr. Rivera pointed to a flier that was posted up front.

"I'll bet it has something to do with this," he told
her. The flier had a picture of a house and said
YOU TOO CAN OWN A HOME.

After our laundry was dried and folded, I took my sister by
the hand and rushed our wagon back to Emerald Street.

At supper I told my parents all about what I had heard and seen. My father scrambled eggs with extra zest, and my mother put ice in our water.

"There's a meeting tonight," I said. "Seven o'clock at the school."

Later on, when my parents came home, they were just as excited as I was.

"This organization buys empty houses and fixes them up like new!" said my mother.

"And if you're interested in helping to fix up a house for other people," my father continued, "then one day other people will help fix up a house for you."

That sounded like a good plan to me. It would be nice to live in a house that wasn't so chilly in winter.

"So we signed up," my father told me. "Can we count on you to help?"

I hugged them so tight I almost fell out of bed. I think they knew my answer.

Well, you know how sometimes, when you never believe that anything will ever be different, then one morning you just wake up and nothing is the same? That's what happened to our family that spring when the project on Viola Street began.

Clang! Bang! Bang! Smash! Those workers started early.

"Take a good look," my mother told us. "That's what we'll be doing soon."

"Are all those people getting a house?" I asked.

"Some of them will," my mother said. "But anyone who wants to can help. It's called volunteering."

Piece by piece, the inside of the first house came apart—one old bathtub, some cabinets, sinks. Slats of wood and piping piled up like a mountain full of junk in the Dumpster.

Most people on the block were happy about the project, but other people were not. The lady next door said, "No banging before nine o'clock!" Some people laughed and said out loud, "Who would want a house in a neighborhood like this?"

But my father would smile and whisper to me, "Sometimes new things are hard to get used to and people are slow to change."

On the weekends, when our family showed up, a leader called out the assignments.

"Everyone here will have a special job to do," she said.

My mother scraped wallpaper off crusty walls that
crumbled like toast. My father and I worked together.
He lifted up old linoleum tiles by sliding a cat-hammer
underneath. My job was to carefully hammer down nails on
the floorboards when he was through.

Some volunteers, like us, hoped to have a house
one day.

"We're looking forward to living in a place without
broken windows and **leaky** pipes," Mr. and Mrs. Rivera said.

My father said he couldn't wait to have a house that
would have heat all winter.

My sisters were still too young to help with all the **construction**. But my mother told them, "Being little is no excuse not to pitch in." She had them squeeze juice from bags of lemons to make fresh lemonade. Then they took turns pouring and passing the cups all around.

At the end of the day there was always a lot of sweeping to do.

"I've never seen so much dust in my life," Mrs. Tran said, covering her nose.

My mother held a dustpan while I pushed the broom. My sisters giggled whenever they saw me wearing my safety mask.

FCAT Essential Message/Theme
Why is the family working so hard?

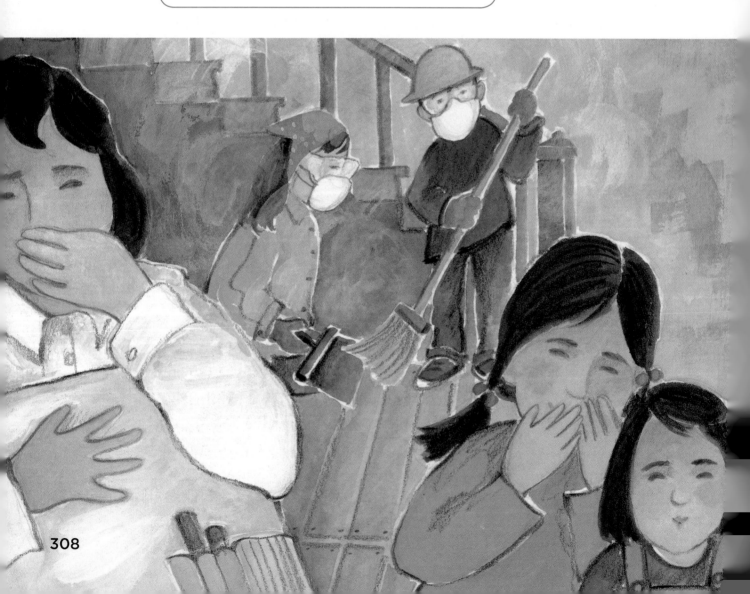

On Saturday nights I'd be so tired, I'd practically fall asleep right after supper.

"You're doing good work," my father would say. And he'd thank me for helping our family. He'd say, "Big dreams are built little by little, and we are making a start."

In those four months I learned a lot about putting things together. Once I even found a piece of wood that my father said I could keep. I thought that maybe I could use it to make something on my own.

One day Mr. Tran gave everyone some news. The new house would be theirs!

"Everything is beautiful," Mrs. Tran said. She stood smiling inside the framed front door. She watched her daughter paint the big front room. The kitchen had shiny linoleum floors and brand-new **appliances**. There even was a washing machine! Upstairs was a bathroom and three carpeted bedrooms. Out back there was a place for a garden.

When the Tran family moved in, they threw a potluck supper. My father and I took care to make something extra special that night.

"Since I've been promoted to cook, I like to whip up a storm," he said.

We not only celebrated the Tran family's being
the **owners** of their new home, but we also celebrated
because we knew we were one house closer to our dream.

Things were really changing on Viola Street now. "This neighborhood looks like it's shaping up," the lady at the Soap & Go said. Volunteers were working on two more empty houses. And of course the Trans next door didn't mind when we wanted to get to work early.

This fall our family was notified that we'd be working on our own house next spring—number one-forty-six Viola Street. Whenever we pass it, my mother says, "I can imagine it finished already." I've already got my bedroom picked out. It's the one with the window by the yard.

During the winter, I made a birdhouse from my piece of wood and gave it to my mother. My mother was more than pleased about that. She said, thanks to me, now even the birds would have a nice little place to call home.

I used to dream that we had a million dollars to buy a house of our own. But in real life all it cost us was a lot of hard work. Anyway, it seems to me like all the money in the world couldn't buy us what we have now on Viola Street. It's just as my father says: Big dreams are built little by little, and we have made a start.

The Nuts and Bolts on DyAnne

Author and Illustrator

DyAnne DiSalvo says that before she starts a book, she can see the whole thing in her mind. Then she gets to work. Sometimes she does research and takes pictures. Other times she just draws a picture she has in her head. DyAnne often uses things she's done to write her books. Just like the characters in this story, DyAnne joined a special group that builds houses for people. She says that her stories are a little bit fiction and a little bit nonfiction.

Other books by DyAnne DiSalvo:
City Green and *A Dog Like Jack*

LOG ON Find out more about DyAnne DiSalvo at **www.macmillanmh.com**

FCAT Author's Purpose

What was the author's purpose for writing *A Castle on Viola Street*? Did DyAnne DiSalvo want to entertain or inform readers? How do you know?

FCAT Comprehension Check

Summarize

Use the Theme Map to help you summarize *A Castle on Viola Street*. Tell about the setting, the characters, and the events.

```
┌──────────┐
│   Clue   │
└──────────┘
      ↓
┌──────────┐
│   Clue   │
└──────────┘
      ↓
┌──────────┐
│   Clue   │
└──────────┘
      ↓
┌──────────┐
│  Theme   │
└──────────┘
```

Think and Compare

READ THINK EXPLAIN

1. Use your Theme Map to identify the theme of *A Castle on Viola Street.* What story details tell about the theme? **Analyze Story Structure: Essential Message/Theme**

READ THINK EXPLAIN

2. Reread page 297 of *A Castle on Viola Street.* What does the mother mean when she says that the family is "rich"? Use story details in your answer. **Evaluate**

3. Which **appliances** in your home are most important to you? Explain. **Apply**

4. What does a family learn from helping another family build a home? **Evaluate**

5. Read pages 292–293. How are the community workers in "What Should I Be?" like the people in *A Castle on Viola Street*? **Reading/Writing Across Texts**

Science

Genre

Nonfiction Articles give the reader information about real people, places, or things.

FCAT Text Features

Textbook features, such as **Introductions**, **Headings**, **Boldface Type**, and **Captions**, help you better understand information in a textbook.

Content Vocabulary

tools

harvesting

mechanical

Pecan Harvesting Tools

by Angel Garcia

Scientists, doctors, students—everyone uses **tools** to do work. Tools, such as forks, help you eat. A computer is a tool that helps you find information.

Tools for Farmers

Farmers could not do their jobs without tools. In Florida farmers produce millions of pounds of pecans every year. It takes a lot of hard work to pick all of those pecans by hand, so special tools help farmers harvest their crops.

Pecans are tasty and heathful, too! They contain fiber, iron, calcium, and many other vitamins that are good for you.

Pecan Farming Tools in the Past

Farmers use tools for **harvesting**, or gathering, pecans. In the 1800s one tool farmers used was a bedsheet. They would put a sheet under a pecan tree. Then they would knock the nuts from the tree with a stick. Once the pecans were on the ground, farmers would wrap them up in the sheets. The sheet was a tool that made picking up the pecans much easier.

Pecan farmers used sheets as a tool to collect and carry pecans.

Pecan Farming Tools Now

Sheets full of pecans were very heavy! Farmers needed better tools for picking pecans. Scientists and engineers in the early 1900s created **mechanical** harvesting machines that made farmwork quicker and easier.

In mechanical harvesting the pecans are gathered using two machines, or tools. The first is a tree shaker. A mechanical arm shakes the pecans to the ground. The second tool rakes the pecans. Using these tools it takes less time and fewer people to harvest the pecan crops.

Farmers use two machines in the mechanical harvesting of pecans. First a tree shaker attaches to the tree and shakes the pecans to the ground.

After the pecans fall to the ground, a tractor rakes them up.

Features in a Textbook

Using Features in a Textbook

The following textbook features are used in this article to help you understand what you are reading.

- An **introduction** is a brief explanation of the main idea of the text.

- **Headings** appear before each piece of writing.

- **Boldface type** calls attention to important words.

- **Different-size type** shows a heading or important words.

- **Captions** explain the photos.

FCAT Connect and Compare

1. Read the captions under the photos with the article. What are the steps in mechanical harvesting? **Using Features in a Textbook**

2. Why did farmers come up with new ways to harvest pecans? **Analyze**

3. Think about the tools that were used in *A Castle on Viola Street*. How did those tools make work easier? **Reading/ Writing Across Texts**

Science Activity

Make a list of the tools that you have used so far today. Which one would be the most difficult to live without? Write a paragraph about this tool.

 Find out more about tools at **www.macmillanmh.com**

Write a Business Letter

Writer's Craft

FCAT Formal Language

Writers use **formal language** with people they do not know well. They use informal language with friends. A good writer uses formal language in a business letter.

I used formal language in my greeting.

I clearly and politely asked for information.

893 Maple Ave.
Elmsville, FL 54321
May 17, 20--

Mr. John J. Garcia
Puppet Playhouse
1 Alton St.
Elmsville, FL 54321

Dear Mr. Garcia:

    I saw Puppet Playhouse perform at a party on May 10th. The performance was fun to watch. Everyone really enjoyed the show.

    I am having a party on June 23rd at 2:00 P.M. Would you be able to perform a fun puppet show for me and my friends? Please send me more information about Puppet Playhouse. Thank you.

Sincerely yours,
Adam Lange

Writing Prompt

People write letters to get information.

Think about some information that you would like to get from a business or organization.

Now write a business letter that explains what you would like to know more about.

FCAT Writer's Checklist

✓ **Focus:** I clearly explain what I would like to know.

✓ **Organization:** My business letter is written in the correct form.

☑ **Support:** I use polite and **formal language**.

✓ **Conventions:** I use punctuation, capitalization, and abbreviations correctly. All my words are spelled correctly.

Talk About It

Animals are amazing creatures. What is the most unusual thing you have ever seen an animal do?

 Find out more about unusual animals at **www.macmillanmh.com**

UNUSUAL ANIMALS

Vocabulary

conversation	scrambled
interrupted	seized
boasting	rebuild
sway	

FCAT **Word Parts**

Prefixes are word parts that come at the beginning of words and change their meaning. The prefix *re-* means "again."

rebuild = build again

MAX
THE AMAZING HAMSTER

by Raymond So

My pet hamster, Max, is really cool and fun. One day while I was feeding Max, my brother Marco came to me with a problem.

"The science fair is next month," he said. "I have to come up with a great project."

"That's easy," I said. "Just build a volcano."

"But everyone makes volcanoes!" he cried. "I want to do something really different."

I could see that our **conversation** about volcanoes was over. I stopped talking, and so did Marco. Finally, I **interrupted** the silence and said, "What about Max? Maybe you could use him for a science project."

"Max!" Marco grinned at us and yelled with delight. "That would be great! Thanks, Mike!"

Marco did some research on hamsters. A few days later, he shared his idea.

"I'm not **boasting**, but I think I've got a really smart project. I'll build a maze. I'll see if Max can go through it faster in the morning or at night. I read that hamsters are more active at night. I think Max will be faster then. Want to help?"

I did! We built a cardboard maze. Then we put a food pellet at one end and Max at the other.

At first, Max started to **sway** back and forth on his little legs, as if rocking like that would help him figure out what was happening. Then, he smelled the food. Max **scrambled** quickly toward it, knocking down a wall as he hurried along. When he reached the food pellet, he **seized** it in his teeth.

"Max did okay, but the maze fell apart!" I said. "Let's **rebuild** it. I'll get some new cardboard."

We made the maze again. The next morning Marco started timing Max. He timed Max twice a day for two weeks—every morning and every night. It turned out that Marco was right. Max was faster at night than in the morning. That little guy is one amazing hamster!

Reread for **Comprehension**

Monitor Comprehension

FCAT **Plot Development** One way to better understand a story is to make **judgments**. To make a judgment, decide whether you agree with a character's **actions**. Use your own experiences to make judgments about the actions. Reread the selection. Use your Judgment Chart to make judgments about the brothers' actions.

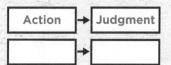

Action	→	Judgment
	→	

Comprehension

Genre

A **Fantasy** is a story about invented characters who could not exist in real life.

Monitor Comprehension

FCAT Plot Development

As you read, use your Judgment Chart.

Action	→	Judgment
	→	

Read to Find Out

How would you describe Charlotte?

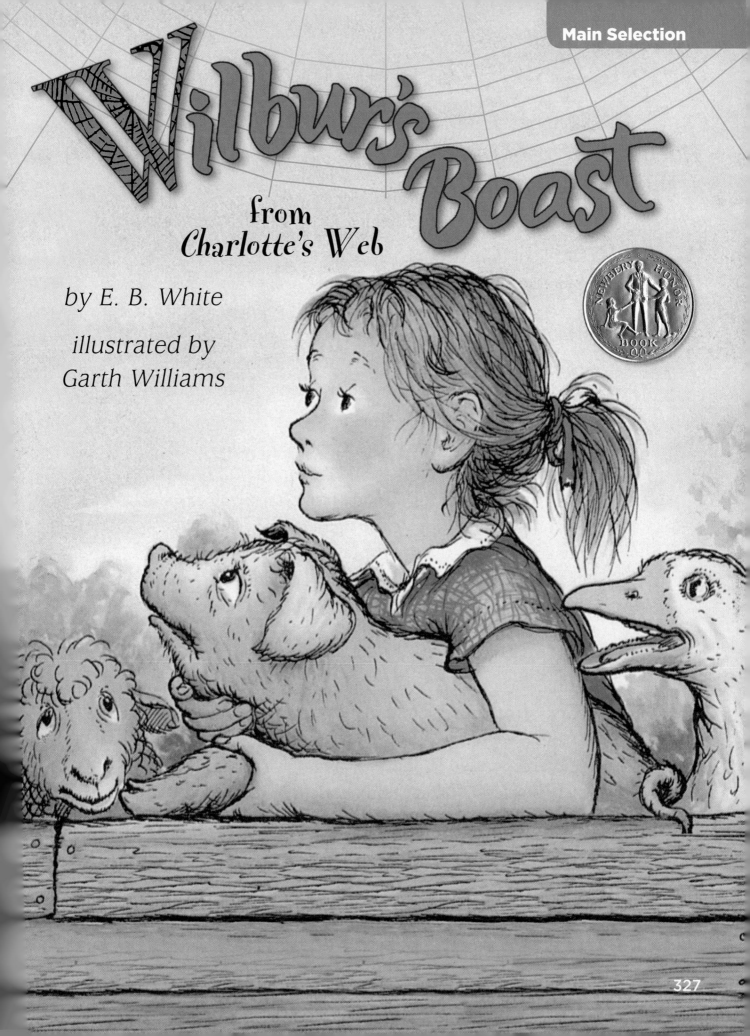

Wilbur's Boast

from
Charlotte's Web

by E. B. White

illustrated by
Garth Williams

A spider's web is stronger than it looks. Although it is made of thin, delicate strands, the web is not easily broken. However, a web gets torn every day by the insects that kick around in it, and a spider must **rebuild** it when it gets full of holes. Charlotte liked to do her weaving during the late afternoon, and Fern liked to sit nearby and watch. One afternoon she heard a most interesting **conversation** and witnessed a strange event.

"You have awfully hairy legs, Charlotte," said Wilbur, as the spider busily worked at her task.

"My legs are hairy for a good reason," replied Charlotte. "Furthermore, each leg of mine has seven sections—the coxa, the trochanter, the femur, the patella, the tibia, the metatarsus, and the tarsus."

Wilbur sat bolt upright. "You're kidding," he said.

"No, I'm not, either."

"Say those names again, I didn't catch them the first time."

"Coxa, trochanter, femur, patella, tibia, metatarsus, and tarsus."

"Goodness!" said Wilbur, looking down at his own chubby legs. "I don't think *my* legs have seven sections."

FCAT Plot Development

How do you feel about Wilbur's comment about Charlotte's legs? What kind of manners does Wilbur have?

"Well," said Charlotte, "you and I lead different lives. You don't have to spin a web. That takes real leg work."

"I could spin a web if I tried," said Wilbur, **boasting**. "I've just never tried."

"Let's see you do it," said Charlotte. Fern chuckled softly, and her eyes grew wide with love for the pig.

"O.K.," replied Wilbur. "You coach me and I'll spin one. It must be a lot of fun to spin a web. How do I start?"

"Take a deep breath!" said Charlotte, smiling. Wilbur breathed deeply. "Now climb to the highest place you can get to, like this." Charlotte raced up to the top of the doorway. Wilbur **scrambled** to the top of the manure pile.

"Very good!" said Charlotte. "Now make an attachment with your spinnerets, hurl yourself into space, and let out a dragline as you go down!"

Wilbur hesitated a moment, then jumped out into the air. He glanced hastily behind to see if a piece of rope was following him to check his fall, but nothing seemed to be happening in his rear, and the next thing he knew he landed with a thump. "Ooomp!" he grunted.

Charlotte laughed so hard her web began to **sway**.

"What did I do wrong?" asked the pig, when he recovered from his bump.

"Nothing," said Charlotte. "It was a nice try."

"I think I'll try again," said Wilbur, cheerfully. "I believe what I need is a little piece of string to hold me."

The pig walked out to his yard. "You there, Templeton?" he called. The rat poked his head out from under the trough.

"Got a little piece of string I could borrow?" asked Wilbur. "I need to spin a web."

"Yes, indeed," replied Templeton, who saved string. "No trouble at all. Anything to oblige." He crept down into his hole, pushed the goose egg out of the way, and returned with an old piece of dirty white string. Wilbur examined it.

"That's just the thing," he said. "Tie one end to my tail, will you, Templeton?"

Wilbur crouched low, with his thin, curly tail toward the rat. Templeton **seized** the string, passed it around the end of the pig's tail, and tied two half hitches. Charlotte watched in delight. Like Fern, she was truly fond of Wilbur, whose smelly pen and stale food attracted the flies that she needed, and she was proud to see that he was not a quitter and was willing to try again to spin a web.

While the rat and the spider and the little girl watched, Wilbur climbed again to the top of the manure pile, full of energy and hope.

"Everybody watch!" he cried. And summoning all his strength, he threw himself into the air, headfirst. The string trailed behind him. But as he had neglected to fasten the other end to anything, it didn't really do any good, and Wilbur landed with a thud, crushed and hurt. Tears came to his eyes. Templeton grinned. Charlotte just sat quietly. After a bit she spoke.

"You can't spin a web, Wilbur, and I advise you to put the idea out of your mind. You lack two things needed for spinning a web."

"What are they?" asked Wilbur, sadly.

"You lack a set of spinnerets, and you lack know-how. But cheer up, you don't need a web. Zuckerman supplies you with three big meals a day. Why should you worry about trapping food?"

Wilbur sighed. "You're ever so much cleverer and brighter than I am, Charlotte. I guess I was just trying to show off. Serves me right."

Templeton untied his string and took it back to his home. Charlotte returned to her weaving.

"You needn't feel too badly, Wilbur," she said. "Not many creatures can spin webs. Even men aren't as good at it as spiders, although they *think* they're pretty good, and they'll *try* anything. Did you ever hear of the Queensborough Bridge?"

Wilbur shook his head. "Is it a web?"

"Sort of," replied Charlotte. "But do you know how long it took men to build it? Eight whole years. My goodness, I would have starved to death waiting that long. I can make a web in a single evening."

"What do people catch in the Queensborough Bridge—bugs?" asked Wilbur.

"No," said Charlotte. "They don't catch anything. They just keep trotting back and forth across the bridge thinking there is something better on the other side. If they'd hang head-down at the top of the thing and wait quietly, maybe something good would come along. But no—with men it's rush, rush, rush, every minute. I'm glad I'm a sedentary spider."

"What does sedentary mean?" asked Wilbur.

"Means I sit still a good part of the time and don't go wandering all over creation. I know a good thing when I see it, and my web is a good thing. I stay put and wait for what comes. Gives me a chance to think."

"Well, I'm sort of sedentary myself, I guess," said the pig. "I have to hang around here whether I want to or not. You know where I'd really like to be this evening?"

"Where?"

"In a forest looking for beechnuts and truffles and delectable roots, pushing leaves aside with my wonderful strong nose, searching and sniffing along the ground, smelling, smelling, smelling ... "

"You smell just the way you are," remarked a lamb who had just walked in. "I can smell you from here. You're the smelliest creature in the place."

Wilbur hung his head. His eyes grew wet with tears. Charlotte noticed his embarrassment and she spoke sharply to the lamb.

"Let Wilbur alone!" she said. "He has a perfect right to smell, considering his surroundings. You're no bundle of sweet peas yourself. Furthermore, you are interrupting a very pleasant conversation. What were we talking about, Wilbur, when we were so rudely **interrupted**?"

"Oh, I don't remember," said Wilbur. "It doesn't make any difference. Let's not talk any more for a while, Charlotte. I'm getting sleepy. You go ahead and finish fixing your web and I'll just lie here and watch you. It's a lovely evening." Wilbur stretched out on his side.

Twilight settled over Zuckerman's barn, and a feeling of peace.

FCAT Plot Development

How do you know that Charlotte wants to make Wilbur feel better? What judgment can you make about her?

336

Spin a Web with
E. B. and Garth

AUTHOR

E. B. White had a farm very much like the one in this story. One day when E. B. was going to feed his pig, he began to feel sad. He did not want his pig to be killed. E. B. thought about how to save him. While he was thinking, he saw a big spider spinning a web. Soon E. B. was spinning the novel *Charlotte's Web*.

Other books by E. B. White:
Stuart Little and *The Trumpet of the Swan*

ILLUSTRATOR

Garth Williams has said that *Charlotte's Web* was one of his favorite books to illustrate. Garth did the pictures while he was living on a farm. He based his illustrations on what he saw around him. He drew the animals over and over again until they seemed to look like people.

LOG ON Find out more about E. B. White and Garth Williams at **www.macmillanmh.com**

FCAT Author's Purpose

What was E. B. White's purpose for writing this story?
How do you know?

338

FCAT Comprehension Check

Summarize

Use your Judgment Chart to help you summarize *Wilbur's Boast*. Tell about an important event in the story and make a judgment about it. Use story information and your own experience.

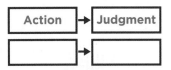

Action		Judgment
	→	
	→	

Think and Compare

1. Make a judgment about Wilbur's **boasting**. Why is spinning a web a good or bad idea for Wilbur? Explain. Include story details in your answer. **Monitor Comprehension: Plot Development**

2. Reread page 335. How does Charlotte feel about humans? Why does she feel her life is better? Use story details and information in your answer. **Evaluate**

3. Suppose you could meet Charlotte. What would you ask her about the meaning of friendship? **Apply**

4. Why does Charlotte explain to Wilbur how to spin a web? **Analyze**

5. Read "Max the Amazing Hamster" on pages 324–325. Compare Max with the animals in *Wilbur's Boast*. Which story is more realistic? Use details from both selections to explain your answer. **Reading/Writing Across Texts**

Science

Genre

Nonfiction Articles give information about real people, places, or things.

FCAT Text Feature

Directions help you follow the steps in a process.

Content Vocabulary

personality

behavior

individual

Do Animals Have Personalities?

by Patricia West

Everyone has a **personality**, or a unique way of acting and thinking. One person might love to run and jump. Another might prefer to sit and think. Your next-door neighbor could be very shy, but your cousin might be friendly to everyone. Each of these people has a different personality.

Animals also have personalities. Scientists study their **behavior**, or the way they act, in order to learn more about them. Here are three **individual** animals that have special personalities.

What a Bell Can Tell

A cat named Phoenix doesn't need anyone to open doors for him. When he wants to go out, he just pushes a special doorbell.

The doorbell's inventor thought that many people would rush to buy cat doorbells, but few have been sold. That might be because not many cats have the same independent personality as Phoenix.

Following Directions

Here's an experiment to find out something interesting about a cat. It will tell you whether a cat is "right-pawed" or "left-pawed."

Is Your Cat Right-Pawed or Left-Pawed?

What to Do

1. Use the spoon to put a little cat food in the bottle.
2. Put the bottle on its side near the cat.
3. When the cat uses its paw to get the food, write down whether the cat uses its right or left paw.
4. Repeat Steps 1–3 several times.
5. Count the number of times the cat uses its right paw and the number of times it uses its left paw.
6. Decide whether your cat is right-pawed, left-pawed, or both.

What You Need

- a hungry cat
- a small, empty plastic bottle with a narrow opening just big enough for the cat's paw
- a little food that the cat likes
- a spoon

341

Pumpkin Play

Scientists at Seattle's Woodland Park Zoo gave carved pumpkins to their gorillas. They observed how their gorillas played with the pumpkins before eating them.

A gorilla called Zuri grabbed as many pumpkins as he could. Another gorilla, Jumoke, spent a lot of time picking out the biggest pumpkin. Alafia looked for a pumpkin she could fit over her head. Congo chose a pumpkin with a face he liked best. Each gorilla showed his or her personality while making choices.

Brilliant Birdbrain

Most parrots can only repeat words their owners say, but one parrot, named Alex, is a talker *and* a good listener! When his owner holds up a tray with different objects, Alex can pick out the yellow object, the biggest object, or even "the one under the square."

Alex also has a good memory. If his owner asks, "Alex, what color is corn?" Alex answers, "Yellow." He can do this even if there is no corn in sight to give him a hint.

FCAT Connect and Compare

1. Look at the experiment on page 341. Explain the directions in Step 4. **Following Directions**

2. Why do you think people like pets with interesting personalities? Explain. **Analyze**

3. How are the animals in this selection similar to the animals in *Wilbur's Boast*? Use details from both selections in your answer. **Reading/Writing Across Texts**

Science Activity

Research an animal with unusual abilities. Write a paragraph that tells about three new things you learned in your research.

 Find out more about unusual animals at **www.macmillanmh.com**

Writer's Craft

FCAT **Transition Words**

Writers use **transition words**, such as *because*, *so*, and *as a result*, to show causes and effects. Transition words make the ideas easy to understand.

I used the phrase "as a result" to connect ideas in the first two sentences.

I used a transition word to connect the sentences.

Write a News Story

Elephant Friends

by Junko N.

Almost 22 years ago, two elephants named Jenny and Shirley performed together in a circus. As a result, they spent a lot of time playing together. Then they were separated.

Recently they met again at an Elephant Sanctuary in Tennessee. Because Jenny and Shirley were old friends, they recognized each other right away. They roared and tried to climb in each other's pens. The people at the sanctuary never saw elephants get so excited, so they put Jenny and Shirley in the same pen. Now the elephants seem happier than ever. After many years their friendship did not disappear.

Writing Prompt

Many interesting stories happen to people and animals.

Think of an interesting story about a person or an animal.

Now write a news story about a person or an animal.

FCAT Writer's Checklist

 Focus: My news story is about one event.

 Organization: I use **transition words** to link my ideas.

 Support: My news story includes facts and details.

 Conventions: I use the correct forms of adjectives that compare. All my words are spelled correctly.

Find out more about citizenship at **www.macmillanmh.com**

GOOD CITIZENS

Pledging Allegiance

October 12, 1892. Do you know the **historical** importance of that date? It was Columbus Day, and on that day 12 million kids in the United States recited the Pledge of Allegiance for the first time.

The original pledge was published in the September 8, 1892, issue of a Boston magazine called *The Youth's Companion*. For years there was a **dispute** over who wrote the pledge. Was it James B. Upham or Francis Bellamy? Both were members of the magazine's staff. Bellamy's son gathered documents and statements to prove that his father was the pledge's author. It paid off. In 1939 the United States Flag Association decided that Bellamy deserved the credit.

THE ORIGINAL VERSION OF THE PLEDGE:

"I pledge allegiance to my Flag and the Republic for which it stands—one nation indivisible—with liberty and justice for all."

CHANGES TO THE PLEDGE:

★ In 1923, at the first National Flag Conference, the words "my Flag" were changed to "the Flag of the United States of America."

★ Congress officially recognized the Pledge of Allegiance in 1942.

★ On Flag Day in 1954, President Dwight D. Eisenhower suggested adding the words "under God." Congress agreed, and the phrase was added.

Becoming a Citizen

Citizens of the United States have certain rights and responsibilities. When people move to the United States from other countries, they do not **automatically** become American citizens. They must fill out an application with the Immigration and Naturalization Service. They must meet certain **requirements**, such as being able to read, write, and speak ordinary English. They must also pass a test on the history and government of the United States. After they become citizens, they have the right to vote and hold public office.

LOG ON
Find out more about becoming a U.S. citizen at **www.macmillanmh.com**

Top 5 States with the Most Hispanics

There are more than 40 million Hispanic people living in the United States. Every year Hispanic Heritage Month begins on September 15, which marks the date when five Latin American countries gained independence: Costa Rica, El Salvador, Guatemala, Honduras, and Nicaragua.

These five states each have a large Hispanic population.

1. California	13,074,156
2. Texas	8,385,139
3. Florida	3,646,499
4. New York	3,139,456
5. Illinois	1,886,933

Source: U.S. Census Bureau estimate, 2006

Comprehension

Genre

A **Nonfiction Article** gives information about real people, places, or things.

Analyze Text Structure

Chronological Order

Some articles are written in chronological, or time, order. Look for dates and signal words, such as *first, next, last,* and *then,* to find time order.

An American Hero Flies Again

How did one astronaut help science twice?

The idea of a person flying into space was a dream until the 1950s. That's when United States and Soviet Union scientists began a space race to make the dream a reality. The Soviet Union pulled ahead, launching two satellites, *Sputnik 1* and *Sputnik 2,* into space in 1957. The U.S. needed a plan to catch up. The National Aeronautics and Space Administration (NASA) was formed to put an astronaut into space. John Glenn would be that astronaut.

John Glenn in 1998

The mission to get a manned spacecraft into orbit was called Project Mercury. Scientists at NASA raced to get a spacecraft ready for launch, but the Soviet Union beat the U.S. again when Yuri Gagarin, a Soviet cosmonaut, orbited Earth in 1961. Ten months later, Glenn climbed aboard the 10-foot-long *Friendship 7* and became the first American to circle Earth in a spacecraft. The U.S. had finally caught up with the Soviet Union in the space race.

Glenn's flight lasted only 4 hours, 55 minutes, 23 seconds from liftoff to touchdown back to Earth. During that time, Glenn orbited Earth three times. It was a historic mission. However, this was not the end of the space race. The next step was getting the first person on the moon. Glenn worked on the cockpit layout and control functions on the Apollo Project. His efforts helped get U.S. astronaut Neil Armstrong to the moon on July 20, 1969.

Glenn was already a hero when he served his country as a fighter pilot in World War II, but at NASA, he was a hero to science. After leaving NASA, Glenn served his country as a U.S. senator. Then in 1998, at age 77, Senator Glenn would get his chance to help science again.

In 1962 an Atlas rocket carried John Glenn and *Friendship 7* into space.

Discovery Mission

NASA scientists needed to find out the best way to study the effects of aging on the body. They needed a qualified older astronaut who was healthy enough to make the trip. That person would also launch a spacecraft to study the heat and winds surrounding the sun. Again, Glenn was chosen.

On board the STS-95 *Discovery*, Glenn wore monitors on his chest and head to measure changes in his heartbeat and brain waves. As people grow older, they experience physical problems, such as loss of balance and muscle tone. The conditions in space have similar effects on astronauts. Because John Glenn wore monitors, scientists today can study the **historical** data of his trip. This data helps scientists to better understand aging.

Ready, Set, Blast Off!

Glenn wasn't **automatically** accepted for the 1998 mission. First, he had to pass physical tests to make sure he was healthy enough. Then he had months of preparation. One of the **requirements** was the ability to save himself in case of an emergency. Glenn admits that he was creakier than the rest of the crew. "I don't bend in the same directions they bend," he said.

Glenn (third from left) and his *Discovery* crewmates

Studying an Aging Astronaut

JOHN GLENN	1962	1998
Height:	5 feet 10 inches	5 feet 10 inches
Hair color:	Red	White
Age:	40	77
THE SPACECRAFT		
Name:	*Friendship 7*	*Discovery*
Crew size:	1	7
Windows:	1	10
Computers:	0	5
Weight:	4,256 pounds	153,819 pounds
THE MISSION		
Name:	Mercury 6	STS-95
Launch date:	February 20, 1962	October 29, 1998
Duration:	4 hr. 55 min. 23 sec.	8 days 21 hr. 44 min.
Distance flown:	75,679 miles	3,680,000 miles

As Glenn got ready to board *Discovery*, thousands of excited fans cheered him on. Among them were Daniel and Zach Glenn, the astronaut's grandsons. "It's a little scary," admitted Dan, 16, "but pretty neat that he went up so long ago and is going up again." Zach, 13, said, "He is a great guy and a really nice grandpa. He's an American hero." There's no **dispute** about that.

FCAT
Think and Compare

1. What happened in the United States after the Soviet Union launched two satellites?

2. What did John Glenn have to do before he was accepted for the 1998 space mission?

3. Why is John Glenn a national hero?

4. How do these selections relate to the theme of "good citizens"?

FCAT **Test Strategy**

Think and Search

The answer is in more than one place. Keep reading to find the answer.

Who Is Uncle Sam?

He has a long white beard. He wears a tall hat and a red, white, and blue suit. He is Uncle Sam—a symbol of the U.S. government. Is Uncle Sam a made-up cartoon character? Or was he a real person?

One idea is that Uncle Sam was named after a man called Samuel Wilson. During the War of 1812, Wilson sold meat to the U.S. Army. The meat was packed in barrels stamped with the letters *U.S.* Some people joked that *U.S.* stood for "Uncle Sam" Wilson.

In 1838 Thomas Nast, a cartoonist, drew a picture of Uncle Sam. Nobody knows for sure where Nast got the idea for this picture. In these cartoons, Uncle Sam has a beard. Samuel Wilson did not have a beard. So Samuel Wilson was probably not Nast's model for Uncle Sam. Thomas Nast was heard saying once that he used himself as the model for the cartoon. The whiskers around Uncle Sam's chin were added later. They were added to make him look like Abraham Lincoln.

By 1916 the United States was at war again. James Flagg painted a poster to get people to join the Army. This poster is the picture we see today. On it, Uncle Sam points and says, "I WANT YOU."

Today, Uncle Sam continues to stand for American strength and determination. Nast never thought his cartoon would become so famous. Even today, his image of Uncle Sam is one of the nation's most known symbols.

Go on ▶

 Now answer Numbers 1 through 5. Base your answers on the article "Who Is Uncle Sam?"

1 Why is Uncle Sam a symbol of the U.S. government?

  Ⓐ He was created long ago.

  Ⓑ Government leaders look like him.

  Ⓒ His picture appears on the U.S. flag.

  Ⓓ He looks determined, and he wears red, white, and blue.

2 James Flagg included all of the following on the Uncle Sam poster EXCEPT

  Ⓕ a beard.

  Ⓖ a tall hat.

  Ⓗ a barrel of meat.

  Ⓘ a red, white, and blue suit.

Tip

Look for key words in the questions.

3 Which statement BEST summarizes the main idea of the article?

  Ⓐ Uncle Sam provided meat for the U.S. Army.

  Ⓑ Uncle Sam was definitely a real person.

  Ⓒ Uncle Sam is a famous United States symbol.

  Ⓓ Government property is stamped with Uncle Sam's picture

4 Describe the making of the Uncle Sam poster. Use details and information from the article to tell how the poster changed from 1838 to 1916. Use time order words in your answer.

5 Describe Uncle Sam's costume. Why might Thomas Nast have chosen the colors and design? Use details to support your response.

STOP 355

Write to a Prompt

FCAT Many people are afraid of things, such as the dark or snakes.
Think of something you are afraid of and the reasons why.
Now <u>tell about</u> this thing you are afraid of and explain why.

Expository writing explains, defines, or tells how to do something.

To figure out if a writing prompt asks for expository writing, look for clue words, such as <u>explain why</u>, or <u>tell about</u>.

Below see how one student begins a response to the prompt above.

The events are told in an order that makes sense.

I am very frightened of spiders. Big, small, brown, and black—they all make me want to scream and run away quickly.

It all started when I was three. My favorite coat was green with yellow snaps. My mom handed me my coat to put on by myself. I felt so grown up because I had just learned how to fasten the snaps. Suddenly, as I was snapping the last snap, I looked down and saw a huge daddy long legs spider crawling across my sleeve! I tore off the coat immediately and started yelling and running around.

That is not the only reason I am afraid of spiders.

Writing Prompt

Respond in writing to the prompt below. Before you write, read the Writing Hints for Prompts. Remember to review the hints after you finish writing.

Communities are full of good citizens.

Think about what a being a good citizen means to you.

Now tell about what being a good citizen means to you.

Writing Hints for Prompts

- ☑ Read the prompt carefully.
- ☑ Plan your writing by organizing your ideas.
- ☑ Support your ideas by telling more about each reason.
- ☑ Use complete sentences.
- ☑ Choose words that help others understand what you mean. Include adverbs that tell how.
- ☑ Review and edit your writing.

WORKING
TOGETHER

Talk About It

How can animals help people at work and at home?

LOG ON Find out more about working together at **www.macmillanmh.com**

Dogs for the Deaf

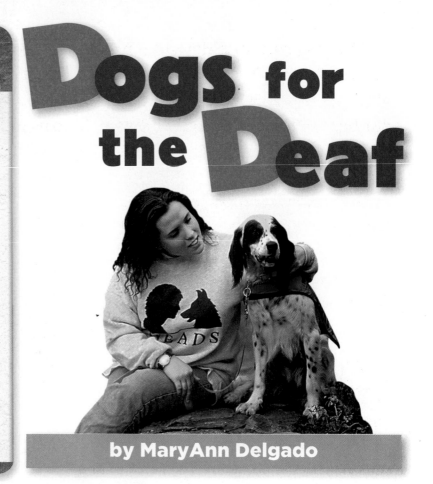

by MaryAnn Delgado

When a fire alarm goes off, you know it! The sound alerts you to danger. What if you were deaf? How would you know if an alarm went off, or if someone knocked on your door? If you took a walk and **strolled** across a busy street, you wouldn't hear if a car beeped at you. A signal dog could help you with all of these things!

Helping Ears

Signal dogs are also called hearing ear dogs. They help people who are deaf by acting as their owners' "ears."

They know what to do when they hear certain sounds. These dogs can learn up to eight sounds, including sounds from sirens, doorbells, and crying babies.

How They Help

Babies cry at night for many reasons. They might be hungry, lonely, or wet. When they cry, the sound is **pitiful**! Even extremely **sleepy** parents will wake up quickly to help. But what if a mom and dad can't hear? That's when a signal dog can help.

The dog can quickly wake his owner. He might nudge him with his nose, or pull at his night clothes. When his owner wakes up, the dog runs to the baby. The dog may **crouch** down near the crib. If his owner doesn't follow, the dog does it again.

The dog will run back and forth until his owner takes action. A signal dog does different things for each sound it knows.

Kinds of Dogs

There is no **official** kind of hearing ear dog. Many sizes and breeds can be trained. Some dogs are short and fluffy. Others are tall, thin, and **sleek**. They may not all move with beauty and **grace**, but all signal dogs are smart!

Large dogs are better in public places because they won't get stepped on. Small dogs, however, can jump in your lap. Why is that important? Because signal dogs are more than just "ears." They are also friends.

Reread for **Comprehension**

Monitor Comprehension

FCAT

Author's Purpose An author writes to entertain, inform, or explain. To figure out the **author's purpose**, you can look for **clues** as you read. Ask yourself, "Is it nonfiction? Does it give information?" You can better understand a nonfiction article if you know to look for important facts and details. Reread the article. Use your Author's Purpose Chart to figure out why the author wrote this article.

Clues

↓

Author's Purpose

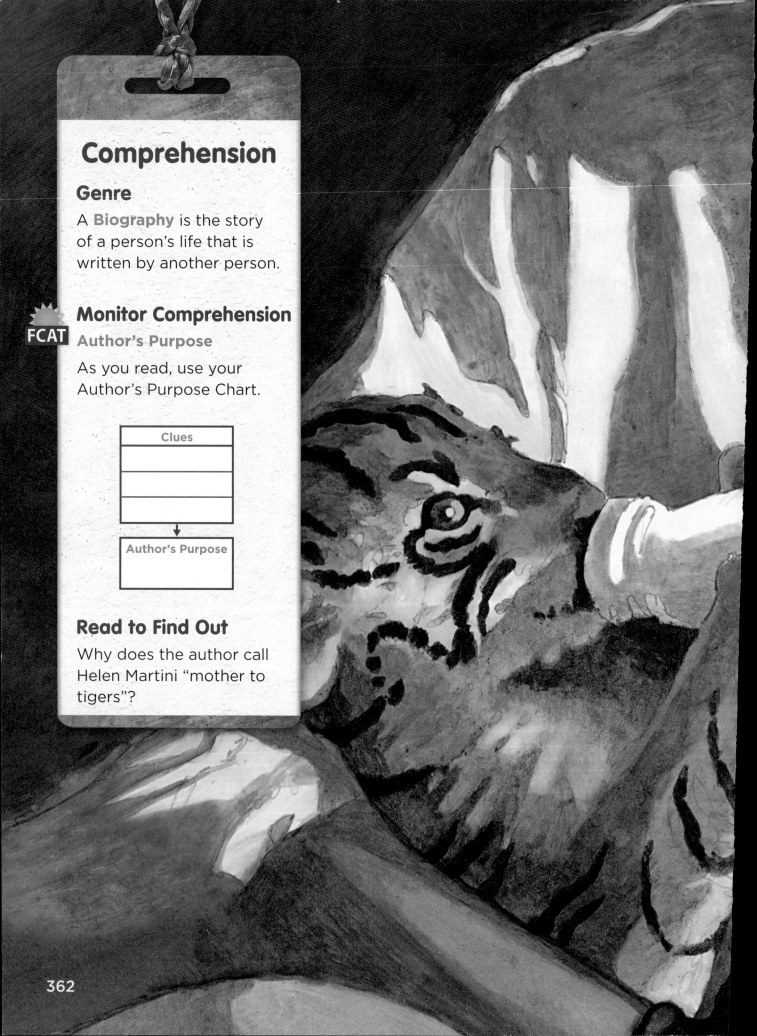

Comprehension

Genre

A **Biography** is the story of a person's life that is written by another person.

Monitor Comprehension

FCAT

Author's Purpose

As you read, use your Author's Purpose Chart.

Clues

↓

Author's Purpose

Read to Find Out

Why does the author call Helen Martini "mother to tigers"?

Mother to Tigers

by George Ella Lyon
illustrations by Peter Catalanotto

Suppose you were a lion cub—abandoned.
Suppose you lay hungry and cold
in the straw at the back of the den,

and a man came in the cage
and lifted you into a case

and put you in a car
to go home with him.

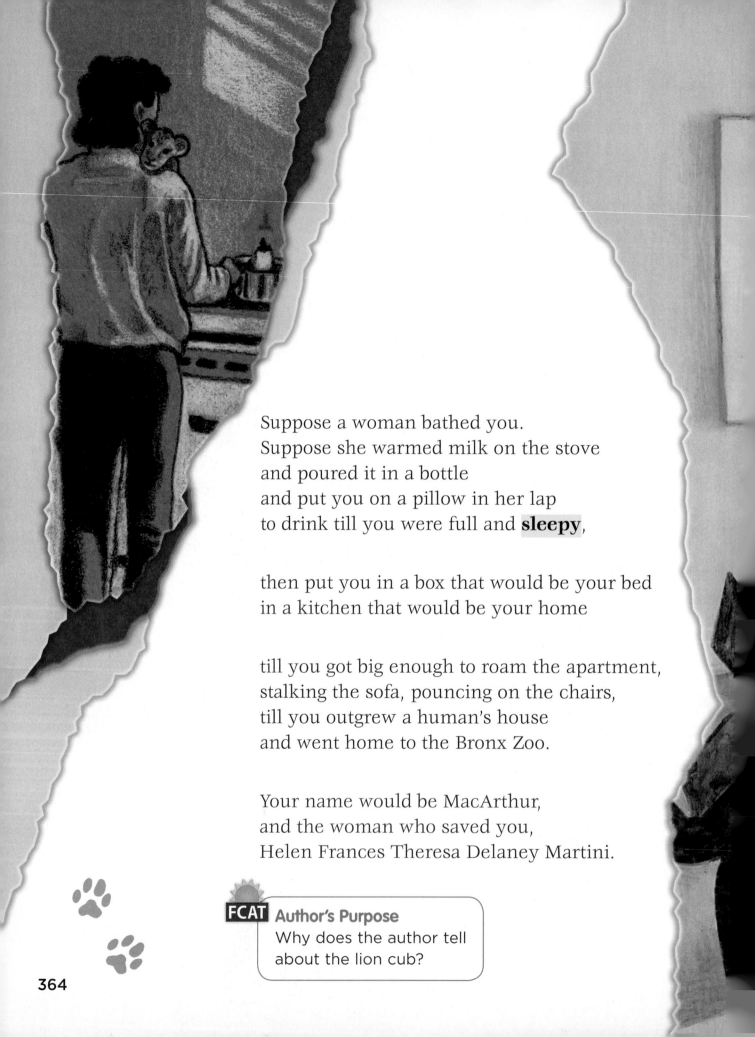

Suppose a woman bathed you.
Suppose she warmed milk on the stove
and poured it in a bottle
and put you on a pillow in her lap
to drink till you were full and **sleepy**,

then put you in a box that would be your bed
in a kitchen that would be your home

till you got big enough to roam the apartment,
stalking the sofa, pouncing on the chairs,
till you outgrew a human's house
and went home to the Bronx Zoo.

Your name would be MacArthur,
and the woman who saved you,
Helen Frances Theresa Delaney Martini.

FCAT **Author's Purpose**
Why does the author tell
about the lion cub?

364

365

Helen never planned to raise cubs.
She and her husband, Fred, wanted children.
But their first baby died,
and doctors said she couldn't have more.

To ease their hurt hearts,
they collected pets: a parrot, a dog,
a starling, and twelve canaries.

Before long, their little apartment
was full of song and feathers.

On weekends, when Fred was free
from his job as a jeweler,
they **strolled** through the Bronx Zoo,
just down the street from their house.

Fred loved those times—
watching polar bears dive
and elephants amble,
studying the **grace** of giraffes.
Finally Helen said,
"Why don't you follow your heart
and work at the Zoo?"
So he did.

Each night he brought home questions
about animals he cared for,
and together he and Helen would read and learn.

When he brought MacArthur home
to the apartment on Old Kingsbridge Road,
the cub was a **pitiful** sight.
"Just do for him what you would do
for a human baby," Fred told Helen.
And she did.

After MacArthur
came Dacca, Rajpur, and Raniganj,
a litter of Bengal tigers.

Rajpur was so cold and thin,
Helen thought he might die,
but she put him on a heating pad
and sat by him for hours
moistening his mouth with milk.
At last he gave a weak cry.
Helen almost cried too.

Feeding three was a challenge!
Helen wished she were an octopus.
But before long those scrawny babies
were **sleek**, fat cubs, ready to romp.

Once, washing clothes in the bath,
Helen heard Raniganj crying.
His head was caught behind a pipe.
While she ran to the rescue,

Rajpur and Dacca discovered the tub.
Crouch ... leap ... *splash!*
Tigers love water.

When the striped trio
had to go back to the Zoo,
they still needed their bottles,
so Helen brought a hot plate
and set up a little kitchen
in the sleeping room
at the back of their cage.

The first night, she and Fred
ate their dinner there too.
Helen didn't want to leave
till her cubs were fast asleep.

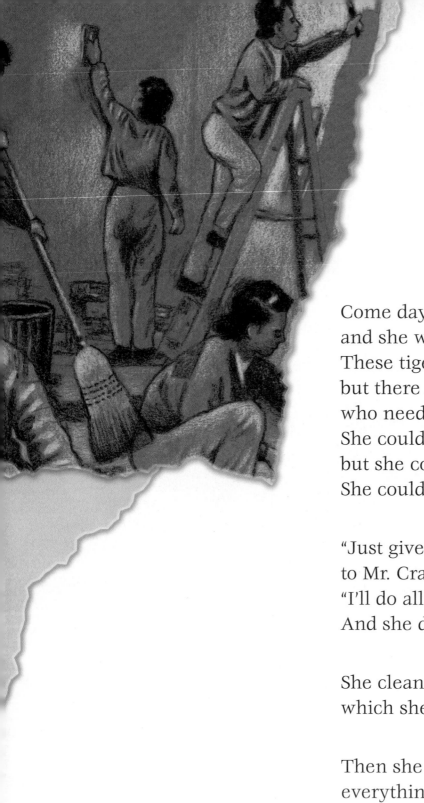

Come daybreak, she was back
and she was thinking:
These tigers will grow up,
but there will always be zoo babies
who need special care.
She couldn't take all of them home,
but she could bring home to them.
She could start a nursery at the Zoo!

"Just give me a room," she said
to Mr. Crandall, the man in charge.
"I'll do all the work."
And she did.

She cleaned and plastered a storeroom,
which she painted pink and blue.

Then she begged, borrowed, and bought
everything she needed.

FCAT **Author's Purpose**
Why did the author
write about Helen?

372

Starting out, she didn't get paid,
but that wasn't what mattered.
She was following her heart,
and her nursery filled up quickly.

Soon it was **official**:
She was the first woman keeper
in the history of the Bronx Zoo.

Before Helen arrived,
no tiger born at the Zoo had ever survived.
She raised twenty-seven,

along with yapoks and marmosets,
gorillas and chimpanzees,
deer and ring-tailed lemurs.

She still took cubs home, too:
lions, tigers,
jaguars, and a black leopard.

Helen's cubs had cubs
that were sent to zoos
all around the world.
The idea of the nursery spread too.

So, wherever you live,
when you go to the zoo,
look hard at the mighty cats.

Their grandparents
may have opened their eyes
on Old Kingsbridge Road,

may have learned to walk
in that apartment kitchen,

saved
by Helen Frances Theresa Delaney Martini,
mother to tigers.

376

377

Roar with George and Peter

AUTHOR

George Ella Lyon first learned about Helen Martini when she was 10 years old. She read Helen's book and began to think about becoming a zookeeper. The next year, George Ella was lucky enough to take a trip to New York and visit the Bronx Zoo. She did not get to meet Helen, but she did see some of her cats.

ILLUSTRATOR

Peter Catalanotto had a lot of practice to illustrate this book. When he was a boy, he spent most of his time down in his basement drawing animals. Today Peter illustrates books by other people and has written some of his own books.

Other books by George Ella Lyon: *Come a Tide* and *Mama Is a Miner*

 Find out more about George Ella Lyon and Peter Catalanotto at **www.macmillanmh.com**

FCAT ## Author's Purpose

What clues from this biography can you use to figure out why George Ella Lyon wrote *Mother to Tigers*? Did she write to inform or to explain how to do something?

"How could such a powerless little mouse ever help me?" That thought made Lion laugh so much that he decided to let Mouse go. A week later, Lion was strutting through the jungle on the way to his napping tree when he stepped onto a hunter's net. The net scooped him up. No matter how he twisted and turned, he couldn't escape.

When Mouse heard Lion's frightened roars, he raced to help. Mouse quickly chewed through the ropes to make a hole in the net. Soon, Lion crawled out and was free.

Lion looked down at the little mouse. "Thank you for saving my life," said Lion, smiling his widest smile. "I was mistaken. You are not a powerless little mouse. You are a great friend!"

Moral: Even the small can show great strength.

FCAT Connect and Compare

1. How are Lion's actions like those of a real person's? Use details from the story in your answer. **Personification**

2. How do Mouse's actions help you understand the fable's moral? **Analyze**

3. Compare the lion in this fable with the cubs in *Mother to Tigers.* How are they similar? How are they different? **Reading/Writing Across Texts**

 Find out more about fables at **www.macmillanmh.com**

Writer's Craft

FCAT A Strong Opening

A good writer knows that a **strong opening** will grab the reader's attention. A strong opening may include a question, quote, or description.

I wanted a strong opening for my article.

I began with a quote to grab my reader's attention.

Write About an Interesting Job

George Chan on Pets

by Trisha M.

"Pets can be wonderful friends, but they are also a lot of work," warns George Chan. How does Mr. Chan know this? He is the director of Clifton's Animal Shelter.

Every year he finds safe, happy homes for hundreds of homeless cats and dogs. His job is to make sure that people take care of the pets from the shelter. He always talks to the new owners before they leave. George Chan makes life better for both pets and people here in Clifton!

Writing Prompt

Some people have interesting jobs.

Think of a person with an interesting job that you heard or read about.

Now tell about a person with an interesting job.

FCAT Writer's Checklist

 Focus: I write clearly about an interesting job.

 Organization: I tell about the job in an order that makes sense.

 Support: I include a **strong opening**. My details tell about the job.

 Conventions: I use commas after introductory words. I use adverbs correctly. All my words are spelled correctly.

Raising Butterflies

Talk About It

Butterflies are born on their own in nature. How can people help them grow?

LOG ON Find out more about butterflies at **www.macmillanmh.com**

Vocabulary

disappear   supply

protect   capture

harming   enclosure

involved

Dictionary

FCAT   **Multiple-Meaning Words** have more than one meaning. Use a dictionary to figure out the meaning of *enclosure* in the last paragraph.

Save Our Butterflies

by Sean Bryant

Scientists who study insects believe that something is happening to our butterflies. They say that 30 years ago, there were about twice as many butterflies as there are today. Where have all the butterflies gone?

The Problem

No one hurts butterflies on purpose. Still, scientists think that people have caused the butterfly problem. Butterflies find their food in wildflowers. When people clear the land for roads and buildings, these flowers **disappear**.

Some insects eat and destroy farmers' crops. Farmers use pesticides, or poisons, to get rid of harmful insects. Pesticides **protect** crops, but sometimes end up **harming** helpful insects such as caterpillars. Caterpillars turn into butterflies. This is another reason there are fewer butterflies now than in the past.

How to Help

Luckily, there are ways that kids and grownups can help. Do you want to get **involved** and help save our butterflies?

One thing you can do is plant a garden. Make sure the garden has a good **supply** of the food butterflies eat when they are caterpillars. Different kinds of caterpillars eat different plants. Monarch butterfly caterpillars eat milkweed. Black swallowtail caterpillars eat parsley, dill, or carrot leaves. Find out what kind of butterflies live in your area and plant the kinds of food they eat as caterpillars. Make sure that pesticides are not used nearby.

One More Thing

Some kids like to **capture** butterflies with nets. Then they put them in a jar or other **enclosure**. Unfortunately, it is easy to hurt a butterfly when you catch it. Its wings are torn easily. Instead, enjoy these beautiful insects from a distance.

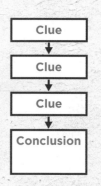

Reread for **Comprehension**

FCAT

Monitor Comprehension

Relevant Details Sometimes readers need to **draw conclusions** about, or figure out, what an author means in a story. To draw conclusions, use details from the story and what you know. By monitoring your comprehension in this way, you will better understand what you read. Reread the selection. Use your Conclusion Map to record **clues**. Draw a conclusion about butterflies.

Clue
Clue
Clue
Conclusion

Comprehension

Genre

A **Nonfiction Article** gives information about real people, places, or things.

Monnitor Comprehension

FCAT

Relevant Facts

As you read, use your Conclusion Map.

Clue
↓
Clue
↓
Clue
↓
Conclusion

Read to Find Out

How have butterflies helped the community?

HOME-GROWN BUTTERFLIES

by Deborah Churchman

People in Barra del Colorado, a village in Costa Rica, had a big problem. For many years, the villagers had caught fish for a living. But then, because of pollution and overfishing, the fish began to **disappear**. Soon it became hard for the people to catch enough fish to feed to their families and sell for money. What could they do?

The village is on the edge of a beautiful rainforest. One thing the villagers could have done was chop down the trees. Then they could have sold the wood and farmed the land. They would have made money but destroyed the rainforest.

A scientist named Brent Davies had another idea about how the villagers could use the rainforest. And it would keep the forest alive. The villagers could raise and sell *butterflies*.

◀ School children in Barra del Colorado are now experts at spotting caterpillars.

▼ Brent Davies and local students admire a sign that notes—in Spanish and English—they are raising insects.

Many colorful butterflies flit around in the forest near Barra del Colorado. It would be easy to **capture** a few and use them to raise many more.

Brent knew that butterfly zoos around the world would pay for farm-raised butterflies. If the villagers could make money by selling them, they'd have a good reason to **protect** the insects' rainforest home. After all, without the forest, there would be no wild butterflies to capture. And without a steady **supply** of wild butterflies, the farm would fail.

Brent wanted to show villagers how to raise butterflies to sell. And she knew just who could help: the school kids! If adults saw kids making money with butterflies, they might want to start their own farm—and protect the forest.

FCAT **Relevant Facts**
What kind of person is Brent Davies? How do you know?

SCHOOLYARD FARM

Butterflies drink nectar from certain flowers, and they lay their eggs on other plants. When the eggs hatch, caterpillars come out and eat those plants. They eat and grow, and grow and eat. When they've grown enough, the caterpillars turn into pupae (PYEW•pee). And those are what butterfly zoos buy.

Brent knew that villagers could find some pupae in the rainforest to sell. But if the people could get butterflies to lay eggs in one place, they could *raise* caterpillars—and get many more pupae.

They could even let some of the extra butterflies they raised go free in the rainforest. That would make sure the forest would always have plenty.

So, how to get started? To attract butterflies, Brent figured the villagers needed a garden full of nectar plants. They also needed an **enclosure** full of plants for caterpillars to eat. She talked to people at the school. Together they decided on a good spot in the schoolyard.

Inside an enclosed area, visitors can see plants grown for hungry caterpillars.

CLEARING AND PLANTING

First they had to clear a lot of trash out of the schoolyard. The kids pitched in and stuffed more than 100 sacks with trash. Soon people were stopping by to admire their work.

Then everyone helped dig up the soil so that plants could grow. That turned up lots of worms—which attracted lots of chickens. So the kids went on "chicken patrol," chasing the birds away. Their butterfly garden needed those worms!

Next, they planted flowers to attract the butterflies. Beside the flower garden, they built the enclosure for raising caterpillars. Then they put the right kinds of plants inside it.

RAISING BUTTERFLIES

Butterflies from the forest flew to the garden to feed on the flowers. Brent taught the children how to capture the butterflies and take them into the enclosure. There, the butterflies laid tiny eggs on the special plants.

Brent also taught the children how to find caterpillars and eggs. (Some eggs are no bigger than the period at the end of this sentence.)

The kids learned to lift up leaves and look around the plants. They put the eggs and caterpillars they found into special feeding boxes. That way they could make sure the insects got plenty to eat.

FCAT Relevant Facts

Why is it important for the kids to find as many eggs and caterpillars as possible?

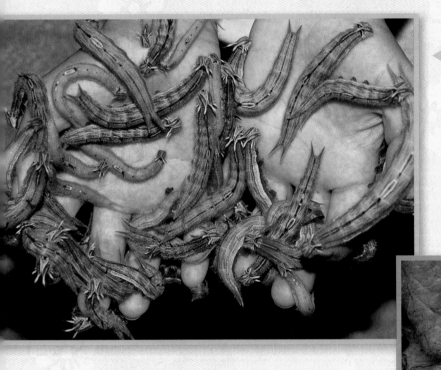

◄ Two handfuls of owl butterfly caterpillars are moved to a feeding box.

After caterpillars turn into pupae, they are ► packed into boxes and shipped to zoos.

Blue morpho butterflies are bestsellers. Their wings have "eyespots" on the underside, but the topside is bright blue.

In the boxes, the caterpillars fattened up on leaves. Then they turned into pupae. The kids picked the pupae just as if they were picking a crop. They let some of the pupae turn into butterflies, and they put those back into the rainforest. But they sold the other pupae.

Today, the farm sells about 250 pupae every month. The money that's earned goes to the school for materials and equipment. The first thing the kids bought was a ceiling fan so their schoolroom wouldn't be so hot!

The best news is that some adults in the village have started doing what the kids have done—making farms for butterflies. They've learned from the kids how to use the forest without **harming** it.

The bottom blue morpho butterfly has just crawled out of its pupae case. The top one has been out for half an hour.

Kids in San Pasqual, California, gather eggs from plants outside their butterfly farm's enclosure.

MEANWHILE, BACK HOME

People at the San Diego Wild Animal Park helped start the butterfly farm in Costa Rica. Then they had another wild idea. Why not start this kind of farm at home in California?

They asked students at San Pasqual Union Elementary School if they wanted to get **involved**. People at the school agreed to do the same thing as the villagers in Costa Rica.

Kids and adults set up a butterfly garden and an enclosed area. Some of the money they earn pays for special things for their school, such as science equipment.

Students from California have started writing to the students in Costa Rica about their butterfly businesses. Both groups of kids feel great about what they're doing for nature!

Charlie Hanscom is just one of the kids raising money for San Pasqual Union Elementary School by helping with the butterfly farm.

FLY AWAY WITH DEBORAH

REPORTER
DEBORAH CHURCHMAN grew up next to a creek in the suburbs near Washington, D.C. Now she grows butterfly bushes and other wildlife-attracting plants in her yard for the enjoyment of her four kids and granddaughter. Deborah is a senior editor at *Ranger Rick,* where she writes articles about nature every day.

 Find out more about Deborah Churchman at **www.macmillanmh.com**

FCAT Author's Purpose

What was Deborah Churchman's purpose for writing *Home-Grown Butterflies*? Did she want to explain how to raise butterflies or to inform readers with this nonfiction article? How do you know?

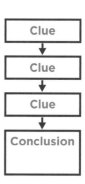

FCAT Comprehension Check

Summarize

Use your Conclusion Map to help you summarize *Home-Grown Butterflies*. Explain how the children were able to help their community by growing butterflies.

Clue
Clue
Clue
Conclusion

Think and Compare

1. How well did Brent Davies's plan work? Use your Conclusion Map and article details to answer. **Monitor Comprehension: Relevant Facts**

2. Reread page 396. Why is it good that the California students write to the students in Costa Rica? Use information from the article in your answer. **Analyze**

3. What would you add to Brent Davies's plan to make it even more successful? **Apply**

4. The people of Barra del Colorado learned how to earn money without **harming** the rain forest. Why is this an important lesson? Explain your answer. **Evaluate**

5. Read "Save Our Butterflies" on pages 386–387. How is this selection similar to *Home-Grown Butterflies*? How are the two selections different? Use details from both selections in your answer. **Reading/Writing Across Texts**

Monarch Butterfly

FCAT

Poetry

Free Verse Poems do not have any regular pattern of line length, rhyme, meter, or stanzas.

Rhyming Poems use elements such as rhyme and rhythm to express feelings and ideas.

Literary Elements

Personification is when an animal or thing has human characteristics in a poem or story.

Assonance is the repetition of the same or similar vowel sounds in a series of words.

The butterfly talks like a person. It also thinks like a person. This is personification.

Wait I can wait
        For the fullness of wings
        For the lift   For the flight
Wait I can wait
        A moment less
        A moment more
I have waited much longer before
        For the taste of the flower
        For the feel   For the sight
Wait I can wait
        For the prize of the skies
        For the gift of the air
Almost finished
Almost there
        Almost ready
                to rise

— *Marilyn Singer*

The Caterpillar

Brown and furry
Caterpillar in a hurry,
Take your walk
To the shady leaf, or stalk,
    Or what not,
Which may be the chosen spot.
    No toad spy you,

Hovering bird of prey pass
    by you;
Spin and die,
To live again a butterfly.

— *Christina Rossetti*

The words *chosen,* *No,* and *toad* repeat the long *o* sound to create assonance.

FCAT Connect and Compare

1. Find an example of assonance in "Monarch Butterfly." **Apply**

2. How does the poet use personification in "Monarch Butterfly"? **Apply**

3. Which stage of a butterfly's life is shown in "Monarch Butterfly"? How did *Home-Grown Butterflies* help you figure this out? Use details from each selection in your answer. **Reading/Writing Across Texts**

LOG ON Find out more about poetry at **www.macmillanmh.com**

Writer's Craft

FCAT Tone

A writer's **tone** may be humorous, suspenseful, or serious. Writers choose precise words to give their writing a specific tone.

I used phrases, such as "whipped furiously," to create a dramatic tone.

Words such as "finally" and "warm" give my ending a positive tone.

A Tale of Two Wings
by Kamryn G.

Our migration has been difficult. Yesterday we flew through a terrible storm. The wind whipped furiously. It tore at my wings. When we stopped to rest, there were no flowers anywhere! What would we eat for energy? Luckily, my tireless sister found a nearby field of flowers. We sipped nectar from the heather, lavender, and aster blossoms. Then we drank water out of big puddles.

It is not easy being a monarch butterfly. Tomorrow we will reach our home in Mexico. Then I can finally warm my wings in the sun!

Writing Prompt

People often like to write stories about animals.

Think about an animal you would like to write a story about.

Now write a story about that animal.

 Writer's Checklist

 Focus: My story is about one idea.

 Organization: My story is told in an order that makes sense.

Support: I choose words that show **tone**.

 Conventions: I use commas correctly. All my words are spelled correctly.

FCAT

Review

Theme
Relevant Facts and
 Details
Problem and Solution
Context Clues
Prefixes
Diagrams

THE NEWS from School

Kevin couldn't believe it when he heard the news. His second-grade teacher, Ms. Blanco, was awarded Teacher of the Year! Kevin decided to write about Ms. Blanco in the school newspaper.

After school Kevin rode his bicycle to Ms. Blanco's house. A group of radio and television reporters waited outside.

"Ms. Blanco, can I talk to you for a minute for the school paper?" asked Kevin.

"I'm sorry, Kevin. I really have no time," Ms. Blanco answered. "I was just telling these reporters that I need to go to teacher-training class."

"Class? Why? You're a teacher!" Kevin cried.

Ms. Blanco explained, "I still take classes every week. In my class I learn more about how to be a better teacher."

Ms. Blanco smiled and rushed away. "How am I ever going to get to talk to her?" wondered Kevin. He thought and thought. Finally, he knew. He would write his questions in a letter. He wrote:

Dear Ms. Blanco,

Congratulations! I'm working on the school newspaper, and I wondered if you could answer a few questions.

1. Did you always want to be a teacher?
2. Do you have any pets?
3. Do you have any hobbies?
4. What advice would you give young people who want to be teachers?

Thanks for your help!

Sincerely,
Kevin Washington

Kevin left the letter under the door of Ms. Blanco's classroom. The next day he found a note waiting for him on his desk. It read:

Dear Kevin,

I'm glad you're working on the newspaper. I'll try to answer your questions.

1. Actually, at first I wanted to be a doctor. It turns out that I can't stand the sight of blood!
2. I have a delightful orange cat named Buster.
3. I love hiking and making crafts.
4. If you want to be a teacher, try to be a good student, and watch how teachers help students learn.

I hope this helps. With your determination, you're sure to become "Reporter of the Year!"

All the best,
Ms. Blanco

A Change in PLANS

The playground at Wilson School has been around for many years. It was just the right size when the school was built. Now the school has many more students, so the playground just isn't big enough.

In October of last year, the Smithville City Council promised to build a bigger playground this summer. The new playground will have more swings, slides, and basketball hoops, as well as a modern jungle gym.

On Monday night the Wilson School Parents Group learned that the playground will not be finished this summer. John Tang, the Smithville City Council President, spoke to the parents. He said that work will start this summer, but it will take a year for the playground to be built. In the meantime students will have no playground.

Many parents were upset. They said that students, parents, and school staff have been looking forward to the new playground for a long time.

Why the Plan Changed

During the meeting one parent spoke up. "Why will it take a whole year to build the playground?" she asked.

Mr. Tang said that construction workers will tear up the old playground during the summer. Then throughout the year, they will work on the playground. Mr. Tang explained that the construction workers are also working on many other projects.

Parents Propose a Solution

The Wilson School Parents Group met again on Tuesday night to talk about the problem. After a few hours, they came up with a solution.

Parents asked the city council to wait until the fall to begin the project. Builders could do the work during the school year. In the meantime the old playground would still be there for students to use this summer. In addition, parents volunteered to donate their time during the year to keep the project on schedule.

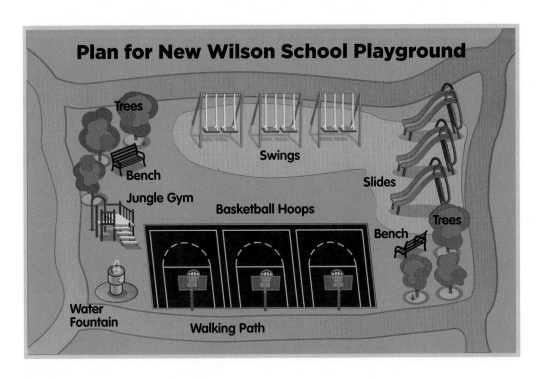

Plan for New Wilson School Playground

Trees

Bench

Jungle Gym

Swings

Basketball Hoops

Slides

Trees

Bench

Water Fountain

Walking Path

Glossary
What Is a Glossary?

A Glossary can help you find the **meanings** of words in this book that you may not know. The words in the Glossary are listed in **alphabetical order**. **Guide words** at the top of each page tell you the first and last words on the page.

Each word is divided into syllables. The way to pronounce the word is given next. You can understand the pronunciation respelling by using the **pronunciation key** on page 409. A shorter key appears at the bottom of every other page. When a word has more than one syllable, a dark accent mark (´) shows which syllable is stressed. In some words, a light accent mark (´) shows which syllable has a less heavy stress. Sometimes an entry includes a second meaning for the word.

Guide Words

First word on the page   Last word on the page

Sample Entry

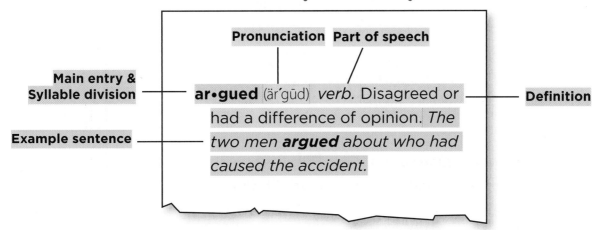

Pronunciation   Part of speech

Main entry &
Syllable division —— **ar•gued** (är′gūd) *verb.* Disagreed or ———— Definition
had a difference of opinion. *The*
Example sentence —— *two men* **argued** *about who had*
caused the accident.

Pronunciation Key

Phonetic Spelling	Examples
a	**a**t, b**a**d, pl**ai**d, l**augh**
ā	**a**pe, p**ai**n, d**ay**, br**ea**k
ä	f**a**ther, c**a**lm
âr	**care**, p**air**, b**ear**, th**eir**, wh**ere**
e	**e**nd, p**e**t, s**ai**d, h**ea**ven, fr**ie**nd
ē	**e**qual, m**e**, f**ee**t, t**ea**m, p**ie**ce, k**ey**
i	**i**t, b**i**g, g**i**ve, h**y**mn
ī	**i**ce, f**i**ne, l**ie**, m**y**
îr	**ear**, d**eer**, h**ere**, p**ie**rce
o	**o**dd, h**o**t, w**a**tch
ō	**o**ld, **oa**t, t**oe**, l**ow**
ô	c**o**ffee, **a**ll, t**au**ght, l**aw**, f**ou**ght
ôr	**or**der, f**or**k, h**or**se, st**or**y, p**our**
oi	**oi**l, t**oy**
ou	**ou**t, n**ow**, b**ough**
u	**u**p, m**u**d, l**o**ve, d**ou**ble
ū	**u**se, m**u**le, c**ue**, f**eu**d, f**ew**
ü	r**u**le, tr**u**e, f**oo**d, fr**ui**t
ù	p**u**t, w**oo**d, sh**ou**ld, l**oo**k
ûr	b**ur**n, h**ur**ry, t**er**m, b**ir**d, w**or**d, c**ou**rage
ə	**a**bout, tak**e**n, penc**i**l, lem**o**n, circ**u**s
b	**b**at, a**b**ove, jo**b**
ch	**ch**in, su**ch**, ma**tch**

Phonetic Spelling	Examples
d	**d**ear, so**d**a, ba**d**
f	**f**ive, de**f**end, lea**f**, o**ff**, cou**gh**, ele**ph**ant
g	**g**ame, a**g**o, fo**g**, e**gg**
h	**h**at, a**h**ead
hw	**wh**ite, **wh**ether, **wh**ich
j	**j**oke, en**j**oy, **g**em, pa**g**e, e**dg**e
k	**k**ite, ba**k**ery, see**k**, ta**ck**, **c**at
l	**l**id, sai**l**or, fee**l**, ba**ll**, a**ll**ow
m	**m**an, fa**m**ily, drea**m**
n	**n**ot, fi**n**al, pa**n**, **kn**ife, **gn**aw
ng	lo**ng**, si**ng**er
p	**p**ail, re**p**air, soa**p**, ha**pp**y
r	**r**ide, pa**r**ent, wea**r**, mo**r**e, ma**rr**y
s	**s**it, a**s**ide, pet**s**, **c**ent, pa**ss**
sh	**sh**oe, wa**sh**er, fi**sh**, mi**ss**ion, na**ti**on
t	**t**ag, pre**t**end, fa**t**, dress**ed**
th	**th**in, pan**th**er, bo**th**
<u>th</u>	**th**ese, mo**th**er, smoo**th**
v	**v**ery, fa**v**or, wa**v**e
w	**w**et, **w**eather, re**w**ard
y	**y**es, on**i**on
z	**z**oo, la**z**y, ja**zz**, ro**s**e, dog**s**, hou**s**es
zh	vi**si**on, trea**s**ure, sei**z**ure

Aa

a·chieve (ə chēv´) *verb.* To do or carry out successfully. *Did Thomas* **achieve** *his goal of cleaning his desk before the bell rang?*

ap·pli·an·ces (ə pli´əns əz) *plural noun.* Small machines or devices that have particular uses, such as toasters, refrigerators, and washing machines. *The store was crowded because of the sale on kitchen* **appliances**.

ar·chi·tects (är´ki tekts´) *plural noun.* People who design buildings and supervise their construction. *A group of* **architects** *showed up at the empty lot and began planning the building they wanted to make there.*

ar·gued (är´gūd) *verb.* Disagreed or had a difference of opinion. *The two men* **argued** *about who had caused the accident.*

art·ist's (är´tists) *possessive noun.* Belonging to a person who is skilled in painting, music, literature, or any other form of art. *The chef uses an* **artist's** *touch when he puts the toppings on his famous desserts.*

au·to·mat·i·cal·ly (ô´tə ma´ti klē) *adverb.* Gets done without a person's control. *Digestion takes place in the body* **automatically**.

ax·is (ak´sis) *noun.* A real or imaginary straight line through the center of a spinning object. *Earth spins on its imaginary* **axis**.

Bb

batch·es (bach´əz) *plural noun.* Groups of things prepared or gathered together. *Tracey and Darryl made several* **batches** *of cookies for the bake sale at the library.*

beamed (bēmd) *verb.* **1.** Shined brightly. *The sun* **beamed** *down on the field.* **2.** Smiled brightly. *Marleigh* **beamed** *when she thought about the joke Raffi told yesterday.*

blos·somed (blos´əmd) *verb.* Grew or developed. *The student kept practicing until she* **blossomed** *into a wonderful violinist.*

boast·ing (bōs′ting) *verb.* Talking with too much pride. *Everyone got annoyed when Lisa started **boasting** about her new bicycle.*

busi·ness (biz′nis) *noun.* **1.** The work a person does to earn a living. *Kenneth worked in the fashion **business** for eight years.* **2.** The buying and selling of things; trade. *The kite shop does good **business** in the summer.*

Cc

cap·ture (kap′chər) *verb.* To catch and hold a person, animal, or thing. *The park rangers were trying to **capture** the bear that was roaming the picnic area.*

clumps (klumps) *plural noun.* Groups or clusters. *After Jennifer went swimming, she had **clumps** of knots in her long hair.*

com·bine (kəm bīn′) *verb.* To join together; unite. *We will **combine** eggs, flour, and milk to make batter for pancakes.*

com·mu·ni·ty (kə mū′ni tē) *noun.* **1.** A group of people who live together in the same place. *Our **community** voted to build a new library.* **2.** A group of people who share a common interest. *The scientific **community** is involved in important research projects.*

con·struc·tion (kən struk′shən) *noun.* The act or process of building something. *It was interesting to watch the **construction** of our town's new grocery store.*

con·tain (kən tān′) *verb.* To hold inside. *The storage boxes **contain** clothes.*

con·ver·sa·tion (kon′vər sā′shən) *noun.* Talk between two or more people. *It was difficult to have a **conversation** with Jerry because of all the loud construction noises.*

---

at; āpe; fär; câre; end; mē; it; īce; pîerce; hot; ōld; sông; fôrk; oil; out; up; ūse; rūle; pu̇ll; tûrn; chin; sing; shop; thin; <u>th</u>is; hw in white; zh in treasure.

The symbol ə stands for the unstressed vowel sound in about, taken, pencil, lemon, and circus.

crate (krāt) *noun.* A box made of pieces of wood. *The grocery store worker emptied the* **crate** *filled with grapes onto the fruit stand.*

crouch (krouch) *verb.* To stoop or bend low with the knees bent. *The firefighters had to* **crouch** *to pick up the hose.*

Dd

de·clared (di klârd´) *verb.* Stated strongly and firmly. *They* **declared** *that they were right and nothing would change their minds.*

de·mand (di mand´) *noun.* An urgent requirement or need. *Katie knew there was a* **demand** *for blankets at the dog shelter.*

de·serve (di zûrv´) *verb.* To have a right to something. *I believe I* **deserve** *to be on the soccer team because I practiced after school and on weekends.*

de·ter·mi·na·tion (di tûr´mə nā´shən) *noun.* A firm purpose. *Miguel's* **determination** *made him study very hard to get the best test score in the class.*

di·rec·tions (di rek´shənz) *plural noun.*
1. Lines leading to a place or point. *The class decided to walk in two different* **directions**: *the boys headed for the lake, and the girls went toward the woods.* **2.** Orders or instructions on how to do something or how to act. *Follow the* **directions** *on the package to cook the soup.*

dis·ap·pear (dis´ə pîr´) *verb.* To stop existing or become extinct. *Elephants began to* **disappear** *because so many people hunted them for their tusks.*

dis·pute (di spūt´) *noun.* A disagreement. *I had a* **dispute** *with my sister about her messiness.*

down·town (doun´toun´) *adjective.* Located in the main part or business district of a town. *My mother works in the* **downtown** *office.*

Ee

en·clo·sure (en klō′zhər) *noun.* A place that is surrounded by a fence or wall on all sides. *The animals were kept in an enclosure until their owners came to pick them up.*

e·quip·ment (i kwip′mənt) *noun.* Anything that is provided for a special purpose or use. *The firefighters showed the class all the different equipment they have and how it is used.*

es·cape (e skāp′) *verb.* To become free. *The students wanted the bell to ring so they could escape the heat of the classroom.*

ex·act (eg zakt′) *adjective.* Very accurate. *I need to know the exact time because I can't be one minute late.*

ex·isted (eg zis′təd) *verb.* Was real. *Tyler couldn't believe that a movie theater once existed where his house now stood.*

Ff

fab·ric (fab′rik) *noun.* A material made from fibers, such as cotton, silk, or nylon. *My mother bought the fabric to make our costumes.*

Word History

Fabric has a complicated history, from the Latin *faber*, meaning "workman," and *fabrica*, "craft" or "workshop," to the Old French *fabrique*, and finally the Middle English *fabryke*, which meant "something constructed."

fled (fled) *verb.* Ran away from something. *Many families fled the hurricane coming toward them.*

Gg

gift (gift) *noun.* Something given to someone, such as a present. *Nigel received a special gift on his birthday.*

grace (grās) *noun.* Beautiful movement, or style. *The dancer moved with grace on the stage.*

---

at; āpe; fär; câre; end; mē; it; īce; pîerce; hot; ōld; sông; fôrk; oil; out; up; ūse; rüle; pùll; tûrn; chin; sing; shop; thin; this; hw in white; zh in treasure.

The symbol ə stands for the unstressed vowel sound in about, taken, pencil, lemon, and circus.

grown·ups (grōn´ups) *plural noun.* Adults. *The children were playing games while the grownups prepared the dessert.*

grum·bled (grum´bəld) *verb.* Complained in a low voice. *The class grumbled when the teacher gave them a lot of homework to do over the holiday.*

Hh

harm·ing (här´ming) *verb.* Doing damage to or hurting. *The construction company was told that it was harming the environment because it cut down so many trees.*

har·vest·ing (här´vis ting) *verb.* Gathering a crop when it is ripe. *Our town farmers begin harvesting pumpkins in August.*

his·tor·i·cal (hi stôr´i kəl) *adjective.* Having to do with history. *This book contains historical information, such as how our town began and a list of its leaders.*

hives (hīvz) *plural noun.* Boxes or houses for bees to live in. *We were warned about the bees and to stay away from the hives in the park.*

Ii

im·age (im´ij) *noun.* A picture of a person or thing. *I still have an image in my head of the beautiful sunset at the beach.*

Word History

Image comes from the Latin *imago*, or *imitari*, "to imitate."

in·di·vid·u·al (in´də vij´ü əl) *adjective.* Single; separate. *The coffee was served with individual packets of sugar.*

in·gre·di·ent (in grē´dē ənt) *noun.* Any one of the parts used in a recipe or mixture. *The baker was missing one ingredient for making a cake.*

in·ter·rupt·ed (in´tə rup´təd) *verb.* Broke in upon or stopped something or someone. *A loud car alarm interrupted our teacher from speaking.*

in·ter·viewed (in´tər vūd´) *verb.* Obtained information from someone by asking questions. *Last night my favorite actress was interviewed on television.*

in·volved (in volvd´) *verb.* Taken up with. *Many students said that they wanted to become involved in raising money for the park.*

Kk

kind·heart·ed (kīnd´här´tid) *adjective.*
Having or showing a friendly or gentle nature. *The **kindhearted** woman put food outside her house for birds to eat during the winter.*

Ll

leak·y (lē´kē) *adjective.* Having a hole or small opening that water, light, or air can pass through. *The **leaky** hose caused a big puddle whenever I tried to water the plants.*

lone·some (lōn´səm) *adjective.* Not often visited by people; deserted. *The **lonesome** house in the swamp was a sad sight.*

luck·i·est (luk´ē est) *adjective.* Having or bringing the most good luck. *Of all the contest winners, James was the **luckiest**; he won the grand prize.*

Mm

mag·nif·i·cent (mag nif´ə sənt) *adjective.* Very beautiful and grand. *We walked through the **magnificent** garden and admired all the beautiful flowers.*

mar·mo·sets (mär´mə zets´) *plural noun.* Small tropical monkeys with claws, soft thick fur, tufted ears, and long tails. *Michael enjoyed watching the **marmosets** at play.*

mass (mas) *noun.* The amount of matter in an object. *The bowling ball's **mass** was greater than the marble's.*

mas·ter·piece (mas´tər pēs´) *noun.* **1.** A great work of art. *The painting Mona Lisa by Da Vinci is thought to be a **masterpiece**.* **2.** Something done with great skill. *Her plan to surprise her brother on his birthday was a **masterpiece**.*

mat·ter (mat´ər) *noun.* Anything that takes up space and has weight. *Water, clay, rocks, and trees are all examples of **matter**.*

at; āpe; fär; câre; end; mē; it; īce; pîerce; hot; ōld; sông; fôrk; oil; out; up; ūse; rüle; pùll; tûrn; chin; sing; shop; thin; <u>th</u>is; hw in white; zh in treasure.

The symbol ə stands for the unstressed vowel sound in about, taken, pencil, lemon, and circus.

meas·ure·ments (mezh´ər mənts) *plural noun.* The sizes, weights, or temperatures of things. *Callie used a ruler to find the measurements of her bookshelf.*

me·chan·i·cal (mə kan´i kəl) *adjective.* Relating to machinery or tools. *Duane bought a mechanical piggy bank that sorts his change for him.*

Nn

na·tive (nā´tiv) *adjective.* Originally living or growing in a region or country. *The cheetah is native to sub-Saharan Africa.*

news·pa·per (nüz´pā´pər) *noun.* A publication printed on sheets of paper that contains news and is published every day or every week. *Many people read the newspaper every morning on the way to work.*

numb (num) *adjective.* Lacking feelings. *The members of the basketball team were numb after they lost the championship game.*

Oo

of·fi·cial (ə fish´əl) *adjective.* Coming from or approved by authority. *The referee announced the official score of the basketball game.*

o·rig·i·nal (ə rij´ə nəl) *adjective.* **1.** Made, done, thought of, or used for the first time; new. *There are not many original ideas coming out of Hollywood anymore.* **2.** Able to do, make, or think of something new or different. *One doesn't need to be an original thinker to watch television.* **3.** Relating to or belonging to the origin or beginning of something; first. *The original owners moved out of the house years ago.*

own·ers (ō´nərz) *plural noun.* People who possess something. *Sarah was very proud that the knitting shop was doing well because she was one of the owners.*

Pp

per·son·al·i·ty (pûr´sə nal´i tē) *noun.* All the qualities, traits, habits, and behavior of a person. *It was in her personality to always be cheerful.*

pitch (pich) *noun.* How high or low a sound is. *Melanie sang the parts of the song that were in a high pitch.*

pit·i·ful (pit´i fəl) *adjective.* Making people feel sorrow for. *The boy standing outside in the cold without his coat looked **pitiful**.*

pos·ses·sions (pə zesh´ənz) *plural noun.* Things that are owned by someone. *Many of his **possessions** were stolen by thieves who broke into his house.*

pow·ered (pou´ərd) *verb.* Filled with the energy to function or operate. *The toy truck was **powered** by batteries.*

pride (prīd) *noun.* **1.** A person's feeling of self-respect, dignity, and self-worth. *Although Rhonda did not score an A in science class, she never lost her sense of **pride**.* **2.** A company of lions. *The antelope were startled by a small **pride** moving in their direction.*

pro·duce (prə düs´ *for verb;* prod´üs *for noun*) **1.** *verb.* To make or create something. *The class was asked to **produce** a play about the signing of the Declaration of Independence.* **2.** *noun.* Farm products, such as fruits and vegetables. *Mom likes to buy fresh **produce** from the farmers' market.*

prop·er·ties (prop´ər tēz) *plural noun.* Qualities or characteristics that can be seen or measured. *Mass and temperature are **properties** of matter.*

pro·tect (prə tekt´) *verb.* To defend from harm. *Mr. Trang put on a heavy overcoat to **protect** himself from the cold.*

pur·chased (pûr´chəst) *verb.* Got something by paying money for it. *Lester's mother **purchased** a bicycle to give to him for his birthday.*

---

at; āpe; fär; câre; end; mē; it; īce; pîerce; hot; ōld; sông; fôrk; oil; out; up; ūse; rüle; pull; tûrn; chin; sing; shop; thin; <u>th</u>is; hw in white; zh in treasure.

The symbol ə stands for the unstressed vowel sound in about, taken, pencil, lemon, and circus.

Qq

quar·rel·ing (kwôr′əl ing) *verb.* Having a heated argument. *My uncles were always **quarreling** about which baseball team was better.*

Rr

re·build (rē bild′) *verb.* To build again or repair. *The farmer wanted to **rebuild** his shed after the storm blew it down.*

rec·i·pes (res′ə pēz′) *plural noun.* Lists of ingredients and instructions for making something to eat or drink. *My mother has many cookie **recipes.***

re·quire·ments (ri kwīr′mənts) *plural noun.* Things that are necessary; demands or needs. *There were certain **requirements** the students had to meet before they could move on to the next grade.*

re·search (ri sûrch′ *or* rē′sûrch′) *noun.* A careful study or investigation in order to learn facts. *A lot of **research** had to be done before the paper could be written.*

Word History

The Old French *recerchier,* which means "to search closely," is where the word **research** comes from.

re·treats (ri trēts′) **1.** *verb.* Goes back or withdraws, as from danger. *A tigress **retreats** when it realizes it is outnumbered.* **2.** *plural noun.* Places to go to for safety, peace, and comfort. *Staying in **retreats** was a helpful way for Bob to leave his problems behind him.*

ro·tates (rō′tāts) *verb.* Turns around. *Marissa's ballet teacher **rotates** perfectly on her toes.*

ru·ined (rü′ind) *verb.* Damaged greatly or harmed. *The flood **ruined** all our carpets in the basement.*

418

Ss

school·house (skül´hous´) *noun.* A building used as a school. *On Friday night, a dance was held at the* **schoolhouse**.

scram·bled (skram´bəld) *verb.* Moved or climbed quickly. *We all* **scrambled** *to the finish line in the three-legged race.*

screamed (skrēmd) *verb.* Made a loud cry or sound. *The woman* **screamed** *when she saw her baby crawling close to the pool.*

seized (sēzd) *verb.* Took hold of or grabbed. *The guard* **seized** *the money out of the thief's hand.*

sep·a·rate (sep´ə rāt´) *verb.* To set apart or place apart. *After the big fight, we had to* **separate** *the cat and the dog and put them in different rooms.*

ser·vi·ces (sûr´vis əz) *plural noun.* A variety of tasks or acts done for others, usually for pay. *The car wash provided other* **services**, *such as dusting and vacuuming inside the car.*

shal·low (shal´ō) *adjective.* Not deep. *All the young children were playing in the* **shallow** *part of the pool.*

shel·ter (shel´tər) *noun.* Something that covers or protects. *Once it began to rain, the group immediately looked for* **shelter**.

should·n't (shüd´ənt) *verb.* Contraction of *should not. You* **shouldn't** *run with scissors in your hands.*

shud·dered (shud´ərd) *verb.* Trembled suddenly. *The house* **shuddered** *during the earthquake.*

side·walks (sīd´wôks) *plural noun.* Paths by the side of the street or road, usually made of cement. *Vladimir and Bill were paid to shovel snow off the* **sidewalks** *around their apartment building.*

---

at; āpe; fär; câre; end; mē; it; īce; pîerce; hot; ōld; sông; fôrk; oil; out; up; ūse; rüle; pùll; tûrn; chin; sing; shop; thin; <u>th</u>is; hw in white; zh in treasure.

The symbol ə stands for the unstressed vowel sound in about, taken, pencil, lemon, and circus.

sleek (slēk) *adjective.* Looking healthy and well cared for. *Everyone admired the **sleek** poodle at the dog show.*

sleep·y (slē′pē) *adjective.* Ready for or needing sleep. *After a big dinner, Raymond felt very **sleepy** and sat down on the couch.*

slo·gan (slō′gən) *noun.* A phrase, statement, or motto. *Today our teacher asked us to think up a **slogan** for our science club.*

sphere (sfîr) *noun.* A round, 3-dimensional shape; a globe. *Each planet is a **sphere** that revolves around the sun.*

sprout (sprout) **1.** *verb.* To begin to grow. *Maria was pleased to see that the sunflower seeds she planted were finally beginning to **sprout**.* **2.** *noun.* A new growth on a plant; a bud or shoot. *There was a **sprout** on the plant that would soon become a leaf.*

stor·age (stôr′ij) *noun.* A place for keeping things for future use. *Mr. Chen used his garage mainly for **storage**.*

strolled (strōld) *verb.* Walked in a slow, relaxed manner. *The tourists **strolled** through the streets looking at all the big buildings and store windows.*

struc·tures (struk′chərz) *plural noun.* Things that are built, such as buildings. *From so far away, the **structures** on the horizon were hard to make out.*

Word History

Structure comes from the Latin word *struere*, which means "to construct."

stur·dy (stûr′dē) *adjective.* Strong or solid. *The new table is very **sturdy**, and we are able to put many heavy boxes on it.*

sup·ply (sə plī′) *noun.* An amount of something needed or available for use. *We had a **supply** of candles and batteries in the closet in case of an emergency.*

sway (swā) *verb.* To move or swing back and forth or side to side. *The trees began to gently* **sway** *in the tropical wind.*

Tt

tast·y (tās′tē) *adjective.* Having a pleasant flavor. *The freshly baked brownies were very* **tasty**.

tem·per·a·ture (tem′pər ə chər *or* tem′prə chər) *noun.* How hot or cold something is. *Jen ate the soup once the* **temperature** *was just right.*

tend (tend) *verb.* To look after or take care of something. *It was the farmer's job to* **tend** *to the cows and chickens and make sure they had enough food.*

ther·mom·e·ter (thər mom′i tər) *noun.* A device for measuring temperature. *The doctor used a thermometer to measure my body temperature.*

thrilled (thrild) *verb.* Filled with pleasure or excitement. *The team members were* **thrilled** *when they heard their best player was not badly injured.*

tools (tülz) *plural noun.* Things that help you do work. *Dad's* **tools** *were stored in a big box in the garage.*

tour (tùr) *noun.* A trip or journey in which many places are visited or many things are seen. *The guide led a* **tour** *through the museum and explained all the famous artwork.*

trad·ers (trā′dərz) *plural noun.* People who buy and sell things as a business. *The* **traders** *went to the settlers to sell them blankets and clothes.*

at; āpe; fär; câre; end; mē; it; īce; pîerce; hot; ōld; sông; fôrk; oil; out; up; ūse; rüle; pùll; tûrn; chin; sing; shop; thin; this; hw in white; zh in treasure.

The symbol ə stands for the unstressed vowel sound in about, taken, pencil, lemon, and circus.

Vv

vi·bra·tions (vī brā′shənz) *plural noun.* Quick movements back and forth. *Jordan plucked the guitar string and watched the* **vibrations**.

vol·un·teers (vol′ən tîrz′) *plural noun.* People who offer to do things by choice and often without pay. *Several* **volunteers** *showed up to help clean up the park and paint the fence.*

Ww

wailed (wāld) *verb.* Made a long and sad cry, especially to show grief or pain. *The baby* **wailed** *when she dropped her toy.*

waves (wāvz) *plural noun.* Curves or ripples. *Our ears pick up sound* **waves** *and turn them into sounds in our brain.*

Yy

ya·poks (yə poks′) *plural noun.* Tropical aquatic opossums with dense fur, webbed feet, and long tails. *The young* **yapoks** *huddled together beneath the shade of the palm tree.*

yearned (yûrnd) *verb.* Felt a strong and deep desire. *The school team* **yearned** *for the chance to play.*

Acknowledgments

The publisher gratefully acknowledges permission to reprint the following copyrighted material:

"Animal Homes" by Ann O. Squire. Copyright © 2001 by Children's Press®, a Division of Scholastic Inc. All rights reserved. Reprinted by permission.

"Beatrice's Goat" by Page McBrier, illustrations by Lori Lohstoeter. Text copyright © 2001 by Page McBrier. Illustrations copyright © 2001 by Lori Lohstoeter. Reprinted by permission of Atheneum Books for Young Readers, an imprint of Simon & Schuster Children's Publishing Division.

"Boom Town" by Sonia Levitin, illustrations by Cat Bowman Smith. Text copyright © 1998 by Sonia Levitin. Illustrations copyright © 1998 by Cat Bowman Smith. Reprinted with permission by Orchard Books a Grolier Company.

"A Castle on Viola Street" by DyAnne DiSalvo. Copyright © 2001 by DyAnne DiSalvo. Reprinted with permission of HarperCollins Children's Books, a division of HarperCollins Publishers.

"The Caterpillar" by Christina Rossetti from BOOK OF POEMS by Tomie dePaola. Text copyright © 1988 by Tomie dePaola. Reprinted with permission.

"A Child's Call to Aid the Zoo" by Jim Davis. Copyright © 2003 by Jim Davis. Reprinted with permission by The Fresno Bee, a division of the The McClatchy Company.

"Cook-a-Doodle Doo!" by Janet Stevens and Susan Stevens Crummel, illustrations by Janet Stevens. Text copyright © 1999 by Janet Stevens and Susan Stevens Crummel. Illustrations copyright © 1999 by Janet Stevens. Reprinted with permission of Harcourt Brace & Company.

"Home Sweet Home" by John Ciardi from THE HOPEFUL TROUT AND OTHER LIMERICKS by John Ciardi. Text copyright © 1989 by Myra J. Ciardi. Reprinted with permission by Houghton Mifflin Company.

"Home-Grown Butterflies" by Deborah Churchman from RANGER RICK®. Copyright © 1998 by National Wildlife Federation. Reprinted with permission of the National Wildlife Federation, May 1998.

"Monarch Butterfly" by Marilyn Singer from FIREFLIES AT MIDNIGHT by Marilyn Singer. Text copyright © 2003 by Marilyn Singer. Reprinted with permission by Atheneum Books for Young Readers, an imprint of Simon & Schuster Children's Publishing Division.

"Mother to Tigers" by George Ella Lyon, illustrations by Peter Catalanotto. Text copyright © 2003 by George Ella Lyon. Illustrations copyright © 2003 by Peter Catalanotto. Reprinted by permission of Atheneum Books for Young Readers, an imprint of Simon & Schuster Children's Publishing Division.

"My Very Own Room" by Amada Irma Pérez, illustrations by Maya Christina Gonzalez. Text copyright © 2000 by Amada Irma Pérez. Illustrations copyright © 2000 by Maya Christina Gonzalez. Reprinted with permission by Children's Book Press.

"The Printer" by Myron Uhlberg, illustrations by Henri Sørensen. Text copyright © 2003 Myron Uhlberg. Illustrations copyright © 2003 by Henri Sørensen. Reprinted with permission of Peachtree Publishers.

"Seven Spools of Thread: A Kwanzaa Story" by Angela Shelf Medearis, illustrations by Daniel Minter. Text copyright © 2000 by Angela Shelf Medearis. Illustrations copyright © 2000 by Daniel Minter. Reprinted with permission by Albert Whitman & Company.

"Think of darkness" by David McCord from MORE RHYMES OF THE NEVER WAS AND ALWAYS IS by David McCord. Copyright © 1979, 1980 by David McCord. Reprinted with permission of Little, Brown and Company (Canada) Limited.

"Wilbur's Boast" (from "CHARLOTTE'S WEB") by E. B. White, illustrations by Garth Williams. Text copyright © 1952 by E. B. White. Text copyright © renewed 1980 by E. B. White. Illustrations copyright © renewed 1980 by Estate of Garth Williams. Reprinted with permission by HarperCollins Publishers, a division of HarperCollins Publishers.

ILLUSTRATIONS

Cover Illustration: Scott Gustafson

12-13: Shane McGowan. 14-39: Janet Stevens. 44: Tim Johnson. 50-73: Daniel Minter. 76: Tim Johnson. 83: Rick Nease for TFK. 84: Jack Thomas. 108-109: Traci Van Wagoner. 110: Tim Johnson. 116-139: Maya Christina Gonzalez. 142: Wetzel & Company. 144: Tim Johnson. 146-147: Sally Springer. 148-149: Wetzel & Company. 154-177: Cat Bowman Smith. 180: Wetzel & Company. 182: Tim Johnson. 188-211: Lori Lohstoeter. 216: Tim Johnson. 221: (tl) Topham/The Image Works. 222: (cr) Mario Ruiz/Time Life Pictures/Getty Images. 234-253: Henri Sørensen. 257: Barb Cousins. 258: Tim Johnson. 282-283: Amy Ning. 284: Tim Johnson. 286: Kathleen Kemly. 294-315: DyAnne DiSalvo. 320: Tim Johnson. 326-338: Garth Williams. 344: Tim Johnson. 354: Library of Congress, Prints & Photographs Division. 362-379: Peter Catalanotto. 380-381: Nicole Rutten. 382: (bc) Tim Johnson. 402: Tim Johnson. 404: Philomena O'Neill. 407: Joe Taylor. 408-409: Lindy Burnett.

PHOTOGRAPHY

All Photographs are by Macmillan/McGraw Hill (MMH) except as noted below:

10-11: Blend/PunchStock. 11: (inset) C Squared Studios/Getty Images. 38: Courtesy Susan Stevens Crummel. 40: (bkgd) Photodisc/PunchStock; (bl) Comstock Images/Alamy. 41: (b) Premium Stock/CORBIS (bkgd) Photodisc/PunchStock. 42: (tl) Foodpix. 43: (bkgd) Photodisc/PunchStock. 44: (bkgd) Wetzel&Company; (b) Michael Newman/Photo Edit Inc. 45: Judd Pilossof/FoodPix/Getty Images. 46-47: (bkgd) James Marshall/CORBIS. 47: (inset) Royalty-Free/CORBIS. 48: (t) Myrleen Ferguson Cate/Photo Edit Inc; (bl) Richard Hutchings/Photo Edit Inc. 49: Myrleen Ferguson Cate/Photo Edit Inc. 72: (tcl) Courtesy Angela Meaderis; (cr) Courtesy Daniel Minter. 74: (bkgd) Don Farrall/Getty Images. 75: (tr) Douglas Pulsipher/Alamy. 76: Royalty-Free/CORBIS. 77: (tl) Tom McCarthy/ Photo Edit Inc; (tc) Emma Lee/LifeFile Photos Ltd./Alamy; (tr) Photodisc/Getty Images. 78: (bl) Peter Lillie/OSF/Animals Animals; (br) Wolfgang Kaehler/CORBIS. 78-79: (t) Michael Gadomski/Animals Animals. 79: (bl) David Hall/Photo Researchers; (br) Doug Wechsler/Animals Animals. 80: Barry Iverson for TFK. 81: (tl) Don Enger/Animals Animals; (tr) W. Perry Conway/CORBIS; (tcl) Nature's Images/Photo Researchers; (tcr) S. Michael Bisceglie/Animals Animals; (cl) Gregory Ochocki/Photo Researchers; (cr) Nigel Dennis/APBL/Animals Animals; (bcr) Photolink/Photodisc/Getty Images; (bl) Stephanie Harvin. 82: Jack Thomas. 83: Joel W. Rogers/CORBIS. 85: Jack Thomas. 86: (cl) Tom Myers/Photo Researchers; (bl) Courtesy Jean Mahoney. 88: SuperStock/AGE Fotostock. 89: (bkgd) Dian Lofton for TFK. 89: (c) Burke/Triolo Productions/Brand X/Alamy. (cr) Tracy Montana/PhotoLink/Getty Images; 90-91: Creatas/PunchStock. 91: (inset) Photodisc/Getty Images. 92: (bl) Peter Kaplan/Photo Researchers. 92-93: (t) Nancy Rotenberg/Animals Animals/Earth Scenes. 93: Heifer International. 94: (bc) Robert Cranston/RJ's Images of Nature. 94-95: (bkgd) Wetzel & Company. 95: (c) Darrell Wong/The Fresno Bee. 96: (bc) Courtesy Stacey L. Caha. 96-97: (bkgd) Wetzel & Company. 97: (bc) Courtesy of The Fresno Bee. 98: (bl) Courtesy Stacey L. Caha. 98-99: (bkgd) Wetzel & Company. 99: (tc) Robert Cranston/RJ's Images of Nature. 100: (tc) David Hunter/The Fresno Bee. 100-101: (bkgd) Wetzel & Company. 101: (bc) Courtesy Stacey L. Caha. 102: (bc) Courtesy Stacey L. Caha. 102-103: (bkgd) Wetzel & Company. 103: (tc) Courtesy Stacey L. Caha. 104: (tc) Courtesy Stacey L. Caha. 104-105: (bkgd) Wetzel & Company. 105: (bc) Robert Cranston/RJ's Images of Nature. 106: (tcl) Courtesy Gary Soto. 106-107: (bkgd) Wetzel & Company. 107: (br) Robert Cranston/RJ's Images of Nature. 110: Superstock/Alamy. 111: (tcl)